# 25 Fun-Filled Collaborative Books Based on Favorite Picture Books

by Phyllis Howard and Mariann Cigrand

NEW YORK • TORONTO • LONDON • AUCKLAND • SYDNEY
MEXICO CITY • NEW DELHI • HONG KONG • BUENOS AIRES

Scholastic Inc. grants teachers permission to photocopy the reproducible pages from this book for classroom use. No other part of this publication may be reproduced in whole or in part, or stored in a retrieval system, or transmitted in any form or by any means, electronic, mechanical, photocopying, recording, or otherwise, without written permission of the publisher. For information regarding permission, write to Scholastic Professional Books, 557 Broadway, New York, NY 10012.

Cover design by Josué Castilleja
Cover and interior illustrations by Rusty Fletcher
Interior design by Norma Ortiz
Edited by Lynn Mondello Caggiano
ISBN: 0-439-32330-4
Copyright © 2003 by Phyllis Howard and Mariann Cigrand.
All rights reserved. Printed in the U.S.A.

1 2 3 4 5 6 7 8 9 10    40    09 08 07 06 05 04 03 02

# Contents

Introduction .................................................................................................... 4
How to Use This Book ................................................................................... 5
Reproducible Lined Paper .............................................................................. 7
**Collaborative Books**
   *Wheels on the Bus* by Raffi ...................................................................... 8

   *I Like Me!* by Nancy L. Carlson ............................................................... 11

   *The Seasons of Arnold's Apple Tree* by Gail Gibbons ............................. 14

   *There's a Wocket in My Pocket!* by Dr. Seuss ......................................... 17

   *If I Had a Gorilla* by Mercer Mayer ......................................................... 20

   *Who Took the Farmer's Hat?* by Joan L. Nodset ..................................... 23

   *Barn Dance* by Bill Martin, Jr. and John Archambault .............................. 26

   *The Biggest Pumpkin Ever* by Steven Kroll ............................................ 29

   *Brown Bear, Brown Bear, What Do You See?* by Bill Martin, Jr. and Eric Carle ............... 32

   *In 1492* by Jean Marzollo .......................................................................... 35

   *Pigs Will Be Pigs* by Amy Axelrod ........................................................... 38

   *"What's in the Sack?"* From *Where the Sidewalk Ends* by Shel Silverstein ........................ 41

   *Sadie and the Snowman* by Allen Morgan ............................................... 42

   *Dear Tooth Fairy* by Kath Mellentin and Tim Wood ................................ 45

   *If the Dinosaurs Came Back* by Bernard Most ......................................... 48

   *The Grouchy Ladybug* by Eric Carle ....................................................... 51

   *Shibumi and the Kitemaker* by Mercer Mayer ......................................... 54

   *Rechenka's Eggs* by Patricia Polacco ....................................................... 57

   *Goggles!* by Ezra Jack Keats ..................................................................... 60

   *Hide and Snake* by Keith Baker ............................................................... 63

   *Tar Beach* by Faith Ringgold .................................................................... 66

   *Dear Zoo* by Rod Campbell ...................................................................... 69

   *The Underwater Alphabet Book* by Jerry Pallotta ................................... 72

   *The Legend of the Indian Paintbrush* by Tomie dePaola .......................... 75

   *Oh, the Places You'll Go!* by Dr. Seuss ................................................... 78

# Introduction

**W**elcome to the world of collaborative bookmaking! These fun and simple early writing experiences use favorite picture books as springboards to create delightful class-made books! First, read aloud picture books by authors such as Dr. Seuss, Patricia Polacco, and Eric Carle. Then invite children to write and illustrate their own page for an adorable literature-based collaborative book.

These 25 collaborative book projects were developed to provide children with meaningful writing experiences. Top-quality literature was selected to motivate kids to write and to provide a model of excellent writing. The books also motivate children to practice reading. You'll find that the collaborative books will become a popular addition to your classroom library. When we used these projects in our classrooms, our students were excited to read their collaborative books again and again.

These projects can be completed as a whole-class activity or as independent activities in writing centers. The collaborative books are easy to connect to your curriculum because they tie in to popular themes such as back to school, seasons, animals, holidays, and more! For each collaborative book, you'll find:
- an adorable reproducible cover template.
- a reproducible student page.
- a teacher page with suggested writing and drawing prompts; tips on preparing the cover, introducing the literature selection, and guiding children through the writing process; and extension ideas and book links.

As each collaborative book was developed and classroom-tested, we found various ways to incorporate meaningful instructional strategies into the process. Refer to the teacher pages and to the section titled How to Use This Book (pages 5–6) for ways to make the most of these skill-building projects.

The open-ended prompts in each project invite children to be creative as they write their responses. Illustrating their ideas also helps beginning writers generate ideas and details for their writing. Finally, adding their page to a collaborative book motivates children to do their very best work. Young writers feel a sense of accomplishment when their work is published and shared with an audience. As your classroom library grows with each additional collaborative book, so will your students' sense of pride in their writing skills.

# How to Use This Book

These 25 collaborative book projects were developed for flexible use. You'll find that there are many ways to incorporate the projects into your curriculum. You might use projects to introduce or wrap up a unit of study (*If the Dinosaurs Came Back*), to commemorate a holiday (*In 1492*), to celebrate a new season (*Sadie and the Snowman*), to teach a genre of literature (*Shibumi and the Kitemaker*), to build a sense of classroom community (*I Like Me!*), and much more. The books tie in to popular themes that will easily take you and your students through the school year. The following suggestions will help the publishing process run smoothly.

## Advance Preparation
Read through the literature selection and the accompanying teacher page in advance. Make photocopies of the cover template and student writing page. Gather any necessary materials such as scissors, crayons, yarn, and other decorative materials. Prepare the front and back covers (see suggestions below).

## Cover Preparation
For greater durability, use a sturdy material for the front and back cover pages, such as oaktag or heavy card stock. Another option is to laminate the cover pages or cover them with clear contact paper. Color the front cover before laminating it. After laminating it, glue on any additional decorations such as movable eyes, ribbon, and yarn. On the inside front cover, write the title of the book you read aloud and the author's name.

Refer to the teacher page for suggestions on preparing the cover. Note that these are only suggestions; feel free to use your own creative ideas or student suggestions to personalize the covers. You might use fabric, stamps, felt, yarn, pipe cleaners, decorative papers, movable eyes, and so on.

## Bookbinding
There are several ways to bind the books. You might simply punch two or three holes along the left side and bind the pages together with yarn or metal rings. For greater durability, use a bookbinding machine. If you use a bookbinding machine, cut along the dotted lines so that the left-hand side of the book is a straight edge. If using other methods of binding, you can either cut along the dotted lines or cut along the solid lines to create a more shaped book.

> **TIP:** For a quick cover, simply photocopy, cut out, and color the cover template. Then laminate it for greater durability. For a more homemade look, trace the cover template onto sturdy paper and cut out the shape. Then write the title, draw your own details using the reproducible as a reference, and glue on additional decorations as desired.

> **TIP:** Punch holes in the student writing sheets before distributing them to children. This ensures that children's writing and artwork will not run into the binding area.

## Exploring the Literature Selections

Refer to the teacher page for specific suggestions for each book. The following ideas will work for any book.

- Before reading aloud the book, show students the cover. Ask students to make predictions about the story, based on the title and cover illustrations.
- Read aloud the summary on the book jacket to prepare students for active listening and spark their interest.
- Together, create a class K-W-L chart (What I Know, What I Want to Know, What I Learned).
- Introduce new vocabulary and concepts.
- While reading, pause periodically to discuss story elements and new vocabulary words.
- Stop at various points in the story and ask children to revise their predictions.
- After reading, ask students follow-up questions, such as "How do you feel about the ending? What do you think happened next? Did you enjoy the story? Why or why not? What was your favorite part? Who was your favorite character and why?"

## Student Writing

Refer to the teacher pages for specific suggestions for each project. Consider the following tips and ideas for any of the projects:

- You may use the prompt provided on the teacher page, or you may adapt the prompt to meet your students' needs. If students need additional support, write the prompt on the student writing page before photocopying it.
- Before students begin writing, work together as a class to complete a sample prompt. Write the prompt on chart paper or on the board and draw a line where the response should be written. Read aloud the prompt and discuss possible responses. Write it on the blank line or have a student volunteer write one. Remind students that there are many possible answers and that they should write their own idea on their page.
- As you complete the sample prompt together, build phonological awareness by discussing beginning and ending sounds of words, rhyming words, syllables, and so on.
- For each collaborative book, create a word bank that children can refer to as they write.
- Model the writing process for students by writing slowly on a surface large enough for the class to see. Discuss grammar, spelling, and other writing concepts.
- Use the projects to practice basic editing and proofreading skills. You might have students complete a rough draft first. Then have them edit and revise before completing a final draft on their student writing page.

> **TIP:** For some projects, it works best to have students write first and then draw an illustration. For other projects, it's better for students to draw first and then write about what they've illustrated. In advance, determine the order in which you would like students to complete their project.

# Reproducible Lined Paper

# Wheels on the Bus

### by Raffi (Crown, 1988)

**I**nvite children along for a ride as a school bus picks up its passengers.

**Themes:** School, Transportation

## Cover Preparation Idea

1. To make front and back covers, trace the cover template twice onto sturdy yellow paper. Cut out the shapes.
2. Using a thin black marker, draw the window frames and other details. Write the title "On the School Bus."
3. Cut out pictures from magazines or use student artwork to add the driver and passengers in the windows.

## Literature

This is the story of a bus that picks up a variety of passengers. The repeating pattern of the text makes it easy for children to join in. Before reading, ask whether students have ever been on a bus. What do they like best about traveling on a bus? What do they like the least? While reading, prompt children to join in during familiar text patterns.

## Writing & Art

Distribute the student writing pages. Write the following prompt on the board "_____ took _____ to school." Students can be creative in coming up with ways to fill in the blanks. If they are stuck, you might suggest that they write their name in the first blank. In the second blank, they could write an object, animal, or person that they would take to school if they had their own bus. In the windows, students can draw a picture of what or whom they brought to school.

## Beyond the Book

- In what ways do students travel to school? Make a graph showing the different forms of transportation that students use.
- Discuss bus safety. Arrange a bus drill to practice safe bus behavior.

**Book Links:** *Bus Stop, Bus Go* by Daniel Kirk (Putnam, 2001). When Tommy's hamster escapes on the bus, an ordinary trip becomes a hilarious adventure! *School Bus: For the Buses, the Riders, and the Watchers* by Donald Crews (Puffin, 1984). A "day in the life" of a school bus (nonfiction). *The Wheels on the Bus, Adaptation of the Traditional Song* by Maryann Kovalski (Joy Street Books, 1987). In this adaptation, a grandmother shares vivid memories of times when she, too, rode a bus and sang this old favorite song.

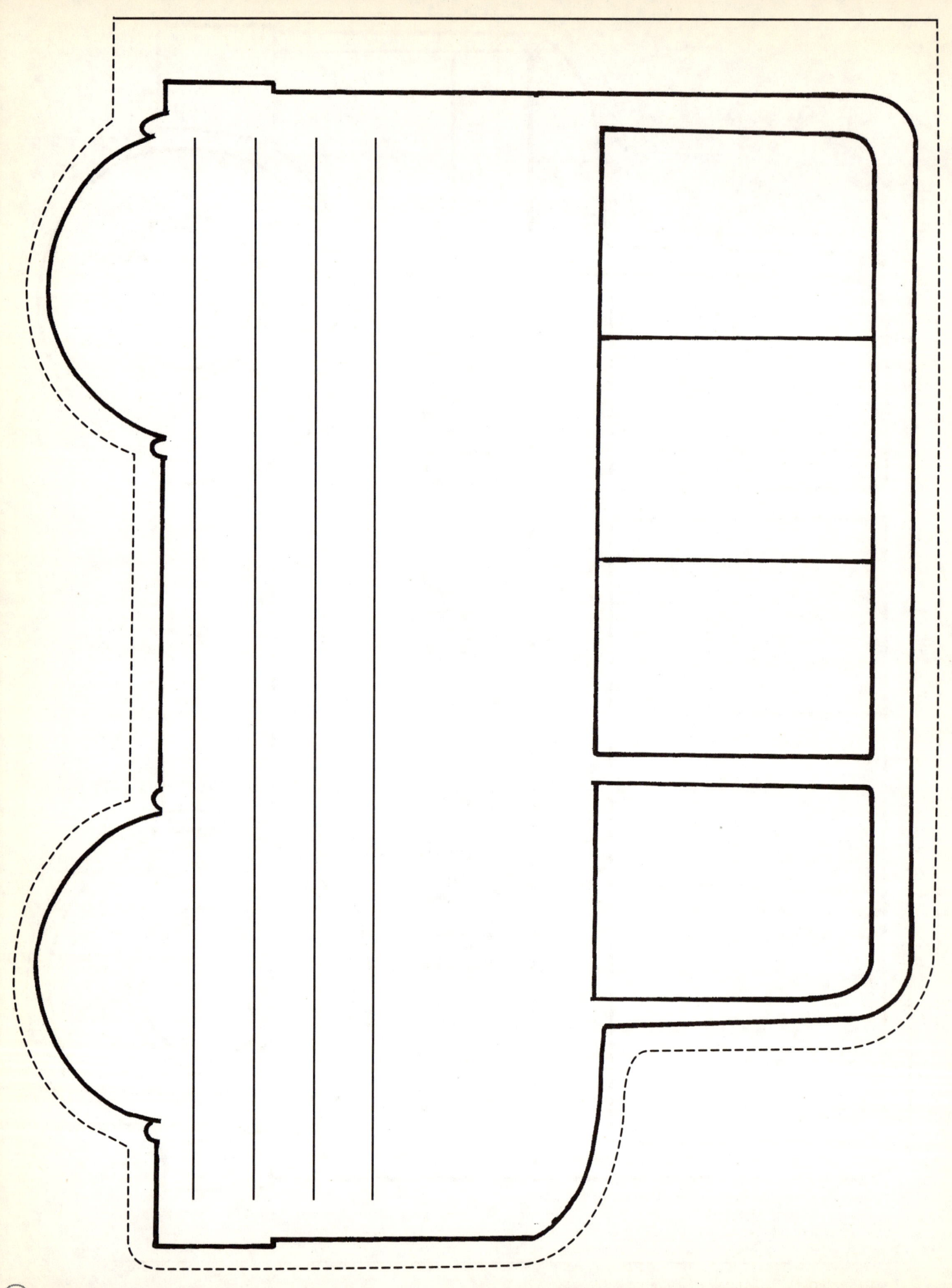

10 Wheels on the Bus · 25 Fun-Filled Collaborative Books Based on Favorite Picture Books

# I Like Me!
### by Nancy L. Carlson (Viking Kestrel, 1988)

Children create a pictograph representing their own positive attributes.

**Themes:** Self-esteem, Individuality

## Cover Preparation Idea

1. To make front and back covers, trace the cover template onto sturdy light-colored paper. Cut out the shapes.
2. Using a marker, add details on the frame and write the title "We're Terrific!"
3. Draw a girl and boy above the title. Or you might cut two figures out of felt and glue them on the cover.

## Literature

In this story, a pig celebrates her individuality as she describes her good qualities and the things she likes to do. Read aloud the title. Before reading the story, share something you like about yourself. Next, have children share something they like about themselves. List students' positive qualities on the chalkboard (friendly, helpful, and so on). After the story, again have children share things that they like about themselves. Did the story help students recognize their own positive qualities?

## Writing & Art

Distribute student pages and invite children to draw a self-portrait in the center. Each child should write his or her name in the box below his or her picture. Provide assistance as necessary. Children can use the remaining boxes to create a pictograph representation about themselves. No words are necessary. Children might illustrate their family, friends, pets, hobbies, strengths, and so on. Children can draw a symbol to represent their quality—for example, they might draw a soccer ball to show that they are athletic.

## Beyond the Book

- Make a pictograph representing your class. Have small groups of students illustrate each class attribute. Include qualities such as quiet workers, kind to others, good friends, responsible, and respectful.

- Ask children to look into a mirror and state one thing they like about themselves.

- Have each child write a self-descriptive acrostic using his or her name.

**Book Links:** *ABC I Like Me* by Nancy Carlson (Viking, 1997). A group of friends describes their uniqueness and talents using the alphabet as a springboard for each describing word. *The Araboolies of Liberty Street* by Sam Swope (Potter, 1989). This lighthearted story of a family who routinely change color and sleep on the front lawn demonstrates tolerance and acceptance. *Big Orange Splot* by Daniel Pinkwater (Hastings House, 1977). After his house is splashed with bright orange paint, Mr. Plumbean changes his way of thinking and learns to celebrate his uniqueness. *Chrysanthemum* by Kevin Henkes (Greenwillow Books, 1991). Chrysanthemum learns to love her unusual name after her parents and a favorite teacher demonstrate all the reasons her name is special.

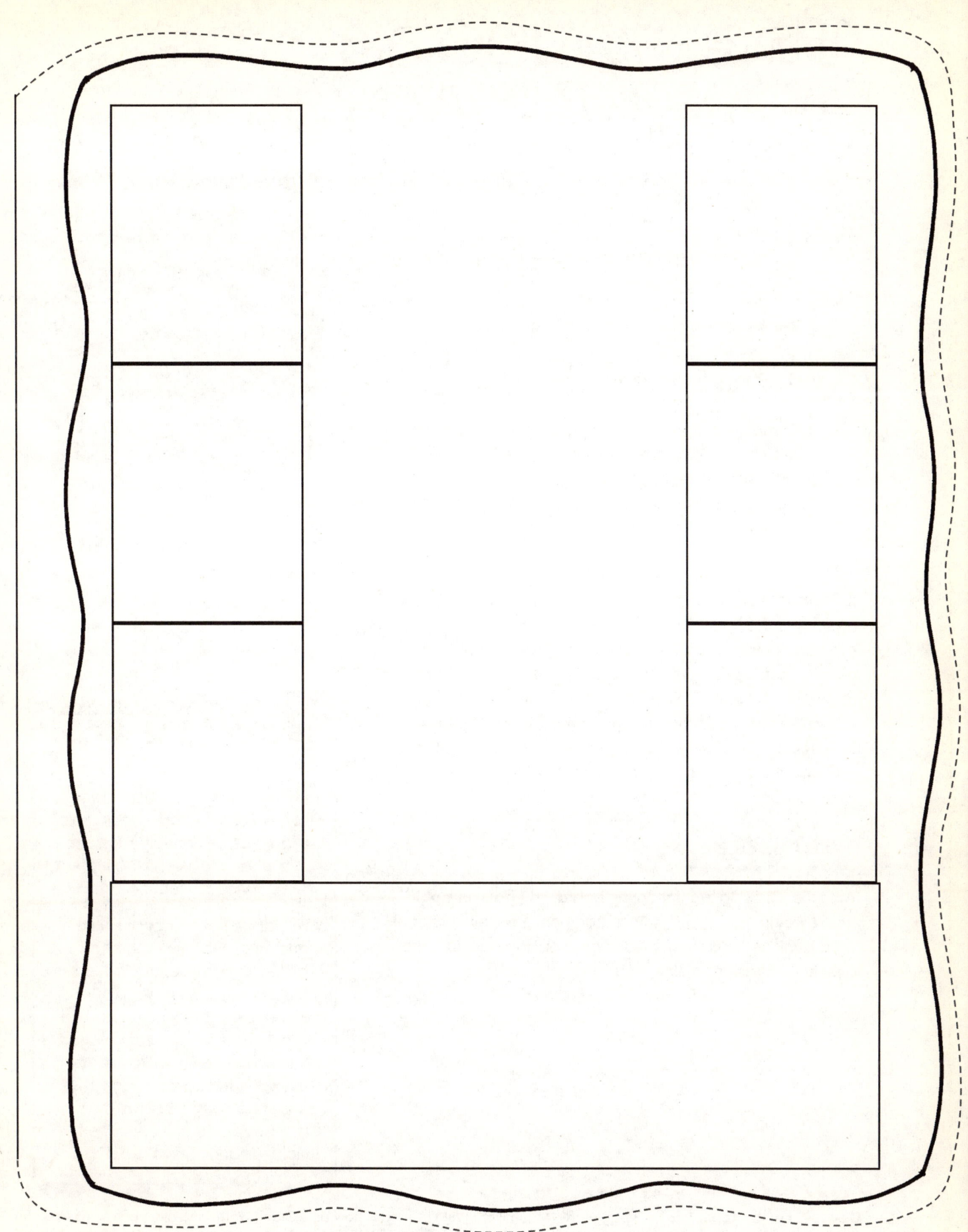

# The Seasons of Arnold's Apple Tree

by Gail Gibbons (Harcourt Brace Jovanovich, 1984)

Children imagine how they would enjoy their own apple trees.

**Themes:** Apples, Trees, Seasons, Cooking

## Cover Preparation Idea

1. To make front and back covers, trace the cover template twice onto sturdy light-colored paper. Cut out the shapes.
2. Write the title "My Apple Tree."
3. Color the tree using markers or crayons. Use a thin black marker to draw details.
4. Attach apples cut from red paper or felt, or use a glue gun to attach red beads.

## Literature

This story shows the ways Arnold enjoys his apple tree through each season. Ask children to imagine that they have their own apple tree. What would they do with their apple tree each season? What would they do with the apples in the fall? Brainstorm a list of ways that they enjoy eating apples. Create an apple word bank on chart paper with words such as *seed, core, seasons, tree, peel, crunch,* and *healthy.*

## Writing & Art

Write the following prompt on the board: **"If I had an apple tree, I would _____."** Encourage children to refer to the word bank as they respond to the prompt. Have children draw a picture to illustrate their writing.

### Beyond the Book

- Make a large tree trunk from brown craft paper and display it on a door or wall. Each season, change the tree to reflect the change of season.

- Cut apples in half crosswise and show children the star pattern in the center. Place the cut apples on a paper towel for about an hour, and pour red tempera paint into trays. Show children how to dip the apples into the paint and then use them to print. Have them try it a few times to determine the right amount of paint to use.

**Book Links:** *Apple Tree* by Peter Parnall (Macmillan, 1988) describes how Little Green Worm and other creatures need an apple to survive. *Cider Apples* by Sandy Nightingale (Harcourt Brace, 1996) tells the story of a girl who saves her grandparents' apple orchard. *The True Story of Johnny Appleseed* by Margaret Hodges (Holiday House, 1997) is chock-full of information about Johnny Appleseed.

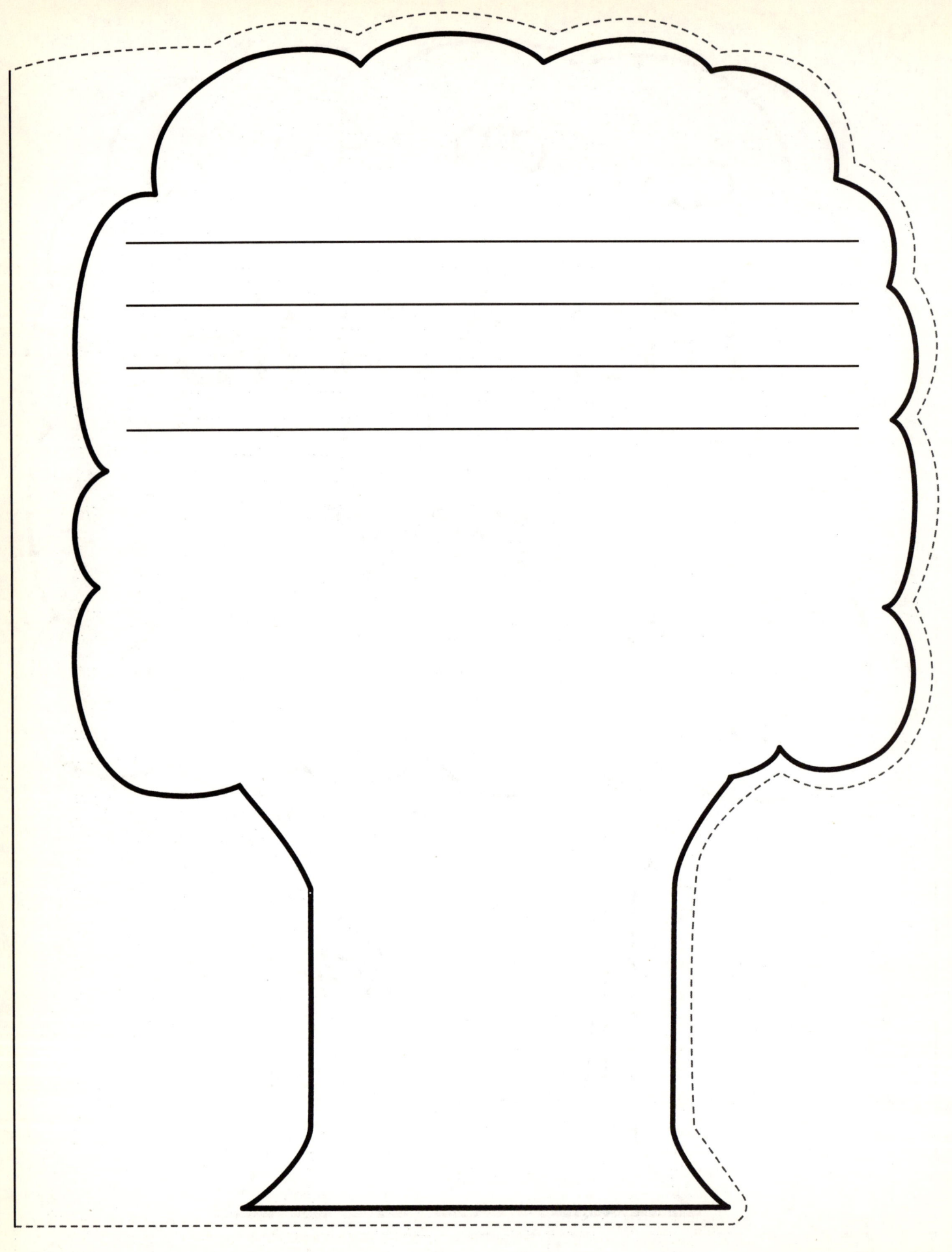

# There's a Wocket in My Pocket!

### by Dr. Seuss (Random House, 1996)

After visiting Dr. Seuss's imaginative world, children come up with their own fanciful idea about what might be in their pocket.

**Themes:** Farm, Animals, Fantasy

## Cover Preparation

1. To make front and back covers, trace the cover template twice onto sturdy colored paper. Cut out the shapes.
2. Trace the pocket onto wrapping paper or other patterned paper and cut it out. Glue the pocket onto the cover. Draw a question mark on it.
3. Write the title "What's in Your Pocket?" in large letters.
4. Color the cover.

## Literature

The narrator tells of the imaginary creatures that live in his house. Each creature's name rhymes with the place in the house where it lives. Pause occasionally before the end of each rhyme to allow children to speculate and say the rhyming word.

## Writing & Art

In advance, cut out enough pockets so that there is one for each child. Cut white card stock into 2- by 2-inch pieces so that you have one card for each student and a few extras. To introduce the writing assignment, ask students what types of things they carry in their pockets. Ask children what they would like to carry in their pockets that might not fit. Encourage students to use their imagination.

## Beyond the Book

- Encourage children to bring pocket-sized items for show-and-tell.
- Classify classroom objects according to size. Discuss what may fit into a pocket and what may not.
- Study kangaroo life; examine how "pockets" help these creatures survive.

Distribute the student writing pages, pocket templates, and white cards. On the white cards, have children illustrate something that they would like to put in their pocket. Then have them complete the sentence prompt **"There's a _____ in my pocket."** Challenge more proficient writers to add details about the object in their pocket. Ask: "What does it look like? Where did it come from?" Encourage children to color their shirts and add a pattern if they wish. Help students glue a pocket onto their shirt. Glue around the sides and bottom of the pocket, leaving the top open. (This is difficult for younger students.) When the glue has dried, show them how to store the drawing of their object in the pocket.

**Book Links:** *A Pocket for Corduroy* by Don Freeman (Viking, 1978). While Corduroy is searching the laundry for a pocket, he encounters several adventures. *Katy No-Pocket* by Emmy Payne (Houghton Mifflin, 1944). A kangaroo with no pocket in which to carry her baby seeks a solution to her problem.

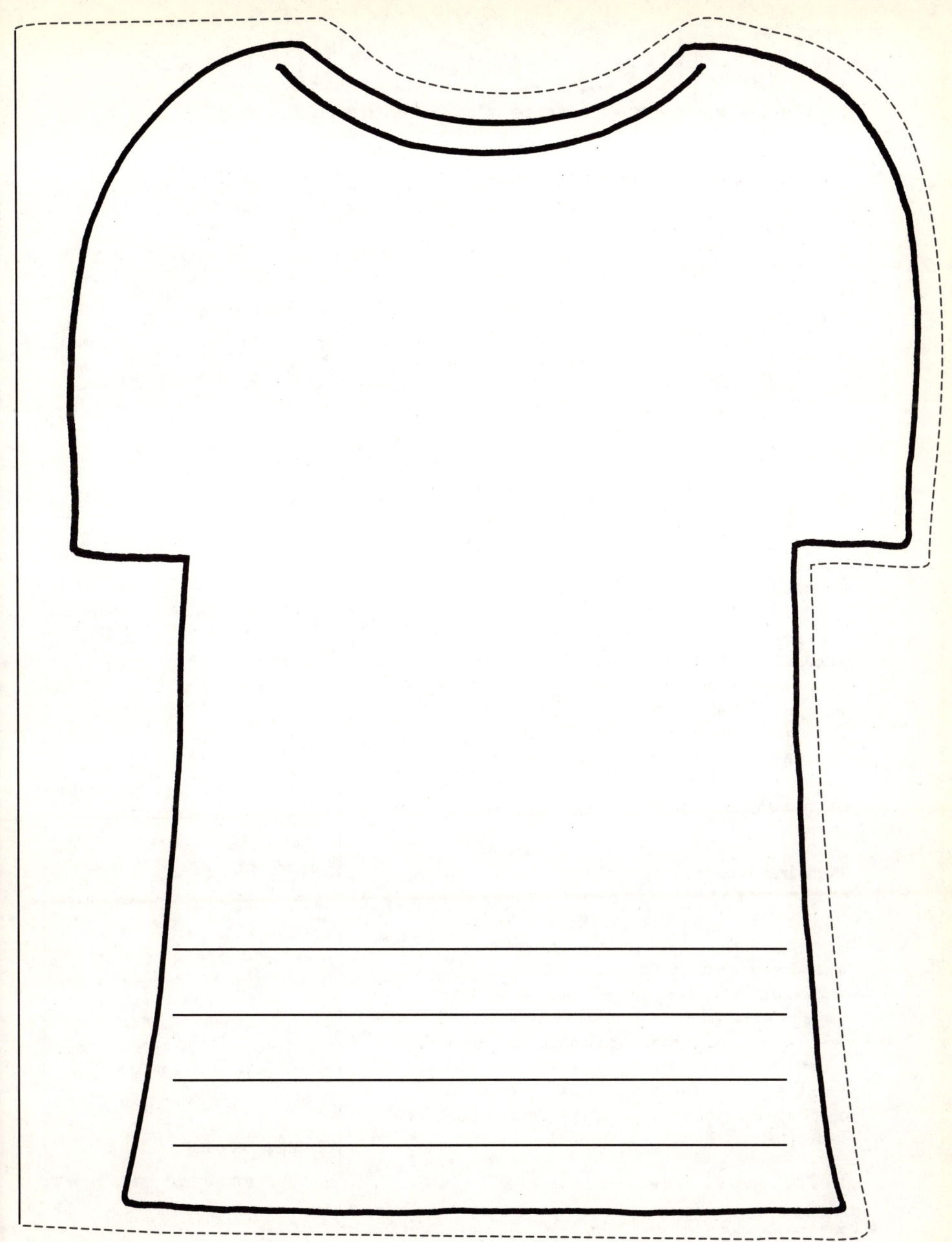

# If I Had a Gorilla
### by Mercer Mayer (McGraw Hill, 2002)

Children use their imagination as they write about what might happen if they had their own outlandish pets!

**Themes:** Animals, Pets

## Cover Preparation Idea

1. Photocopy the cover template twice onto yellow paper. Mount one copy on sturdy paper and cut it out. For the back cover, trace onto sturdy paper and cut out the shape.
2. Using the extra copy of the cover template, cut around the lion's mane. Trace onto yellow or orange felt and cut it out. Glue the felt onto the cover.
3. Cut out the lion's face from the template in step 2 and glue it onto the center of the mane. You might add movable eyes and pipe cleaners for whiskers.

## Literature

In this story, a boy thinks about what he would do if he had various animals. Each idea is presented in an *If ... I'd ... Then ...* pattern. Read the title and ask children to predict what the story might be about. After reading the first few passages, pause before reading the patterned statements. Invite students to help you read each passage, or ask students to make predictions about what they think the narrator will think of next. Familiarity with the story pattern as well as illustrations should guide student attempts.

## Writing & Art

Write the following prompts on the board **"If I had a _____, I'd _____. Then _____."** Tell students that you would like to have a lion for your classroom. Together fill in the prompt. Think of what you'd have the lion do and what the results would be. Fill in a student page with this information and use it as the first page in the collaborative book. Encourage students to think about an unusual pet that they might like to have. Distribute student writing pages and provide guidance as children are writing. Invite students to draw a picture of their unusual pet.

## Beyond the Book

- Talk about what it means to be responsible. What are some things for which your students are responsible? What responsibilities *do* they like the best? Which do they like the least? Poll the class and chart their responses.

- Discuss the responsibilities of a pet owner. List the virtues of common pets. Is it worth the work to have a pet?

- Have students share stories about their own pets or those of friends. Invite them to bring in photos or draw pictures. Create a bulletin board of "Animal Friends."

**Book Links:** *A to Z Beastly Jamboree* by Robert Bender (Lodestar Books/Dutton, 1996). In this alliterative story, each animal performs an action that begins with the same letter as its name. *Can I Keep Him?* by Steven Kellog (Dial, 1971). Arnold brings home potential pet after pet, but his mother's response is the same to all—except one. *"Let's Get a Pup," Said Kate* by Bob Graham (Candlewick Press, 2001). After the death of her cat, Kate suggests getting a pup. Her family agrees, but they end up with one more dog than they had bargained for.

# Who Took the Farmer's Hat?

**by Joan L. Nodset (Harper & Row, 1963)**

After learning about how the farm animals made use of the farmer's hat, children imagine who might make use of their own hat.

**Themes:** Farm, Hats

## Cover Preparation Idea

1. To make front and back covers, trace the cover template twice onto sturdy light-colored paper. Cut out the shapes.
2. Glue a ribbon or colorful fabric for the band, if desired.
3. Write the title "Who Took My Hat?"
4. Finish by gluing a feather onto the band.

## Literature

When the wind blows a farmer's hat off his head, the animals on the farm use it in many unusual ways. Using the cover illustrations as a guide, ask children to predict who they think took the farmer's hat.

## Writing & Art

Ask students to imagine that they had a favorite hat that was taken away. Pass out the student writing pages and have them tell their own story in the space provided. You might start them off by writing the following prompt on the board: "_____ **took my hat.**" Encourage students to include who took their hat, what it was used for, what happened to it, and how they felt about it. When they have finished, encourage students to draw an illustration to support their writing.

## Beyond the Book

- Choose a day that will become Hat Day. Encourage children to bring in a favorite hat from home or to make their own interesting hat in school.

- Make a bulletin board with the title "Hats Off to Reading!" On the bulletin baord, write the titles of the books students are reading. Have students wear their special hats during independent reading time.

**Book Links:** *Caps for Sale* by Esphyr Slobodkina (W. R. Scott, 1940) tells the story of a peddler and the mischievous monkeys that steal his caps. *Curious George Rides a Bike* by H. A. Rey (Houghton Mifflin, 1952). George helps a boy with his paper route and finds himself in all sorts of trouble. As an added bonus, this story shows how to make a newspaper hat.

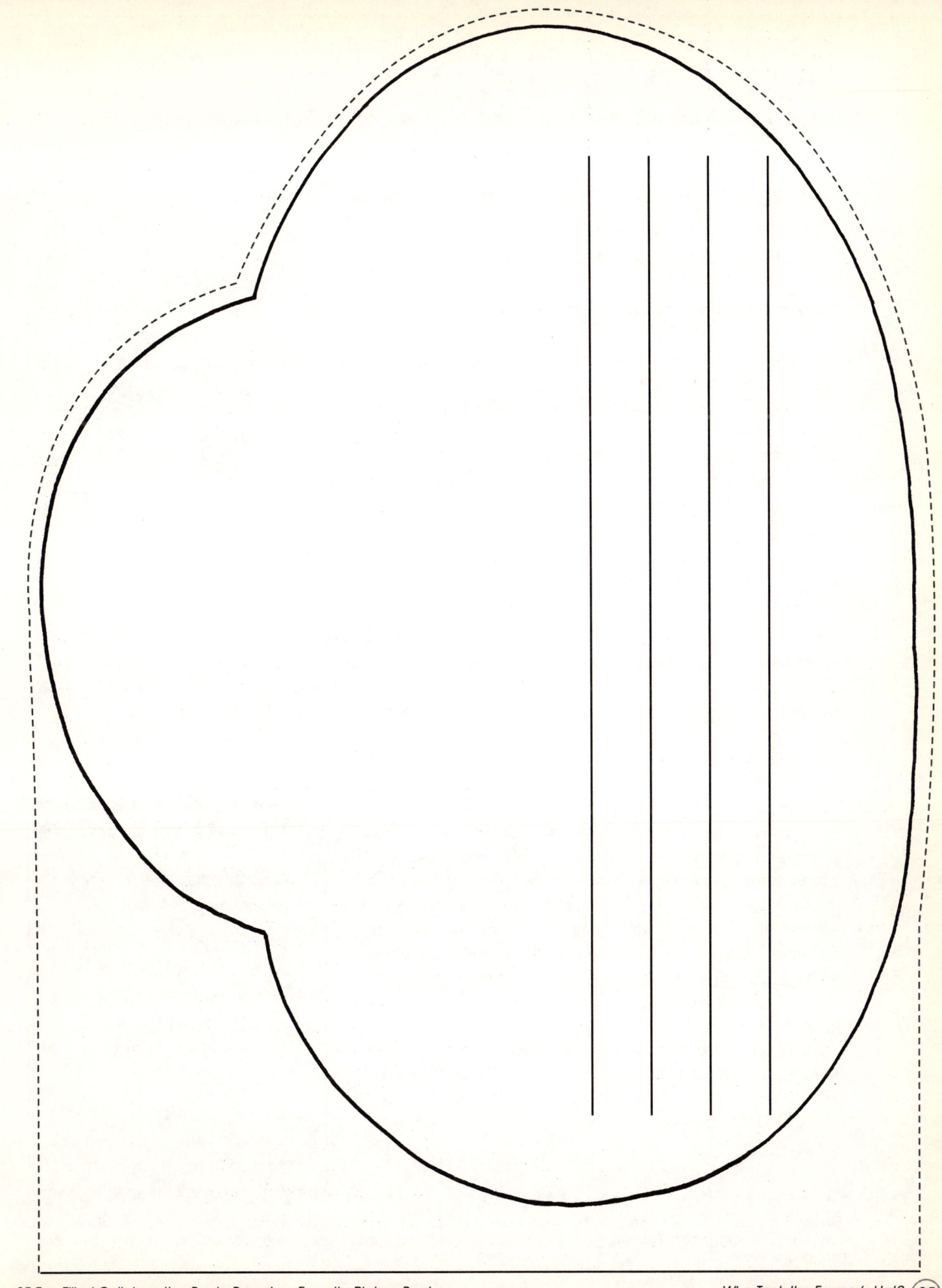

# Barn Dance

by Bill Martin, Jr. and John Archambault (Henry Holt, 1986)

**I**nvite children to take part in an imaginary barn dance with this magical story.

**Themes:** Farm, Animals, Fantasy

## Cover Preparation Idea

1. Photocopy the cover template onto red paper. Cut the doors along the dotted lines and fold them back.
2. Mount onto sturdy white paper without gluing the doors. Cut out the shape, leaving the white paper behind the doors. For the back cover, trace onto sturdy paper and cut out.
3. Invite a child to draw a farmer and animals in the doorway on the front cover.
4. Glue hay, broom straws, or Spanish moss onto the cover.

## Literature

In this story, a boy follows a voice that leads him into a barn. In the magic of the night, the animals are having a dance inside. Before reading the book, show students the cover and ask them what they think a barn dance would be like. After reading, review the animals that were included in the story and write them on the board or on chart paper. Ask children what they know about each animal's features and habits.

## Writing & Art

In advance, cut 5- by 5-inch squares of white paper. Make a copy of the student writing page for each student. Cut the doors so that they open like two flaps, and tape or glue a paper square in the opening. Invite children to imagine that they are at the barn dance. What would they see? Whom would they dance with? What kind of music would they hear? Then write one of the following writing prompts on the board: **"I danced in the barn with _____."** (for beginning writers) or **"At the barn dance, _____."** (for more advanced writers).

Have students write their responses on the lines above the doors. Then have them color the rest of the barn. Explain that students will fold back the door flaps and draw a picture of themselves and their dance partner.

## Beyond the Book

- Make a graph of the animals children wrote about.
- Have students each research the animal they wrote about. Then have students write one or two interesting facts to share and then display on a bulletin board.
- Read a nonfiction book about farms. Compare and contrast the books as a group activity.

**Book Links:** *A Farmer's Alphabet* by Mary Azarian (Godine, 1984) features beautiful woodcut illustrations of farm life for each letter of the alphabet. *Farming* by Gail Gibbons (Holiday, 1988) provides a simple and colorful introduction to farming through the seasons.

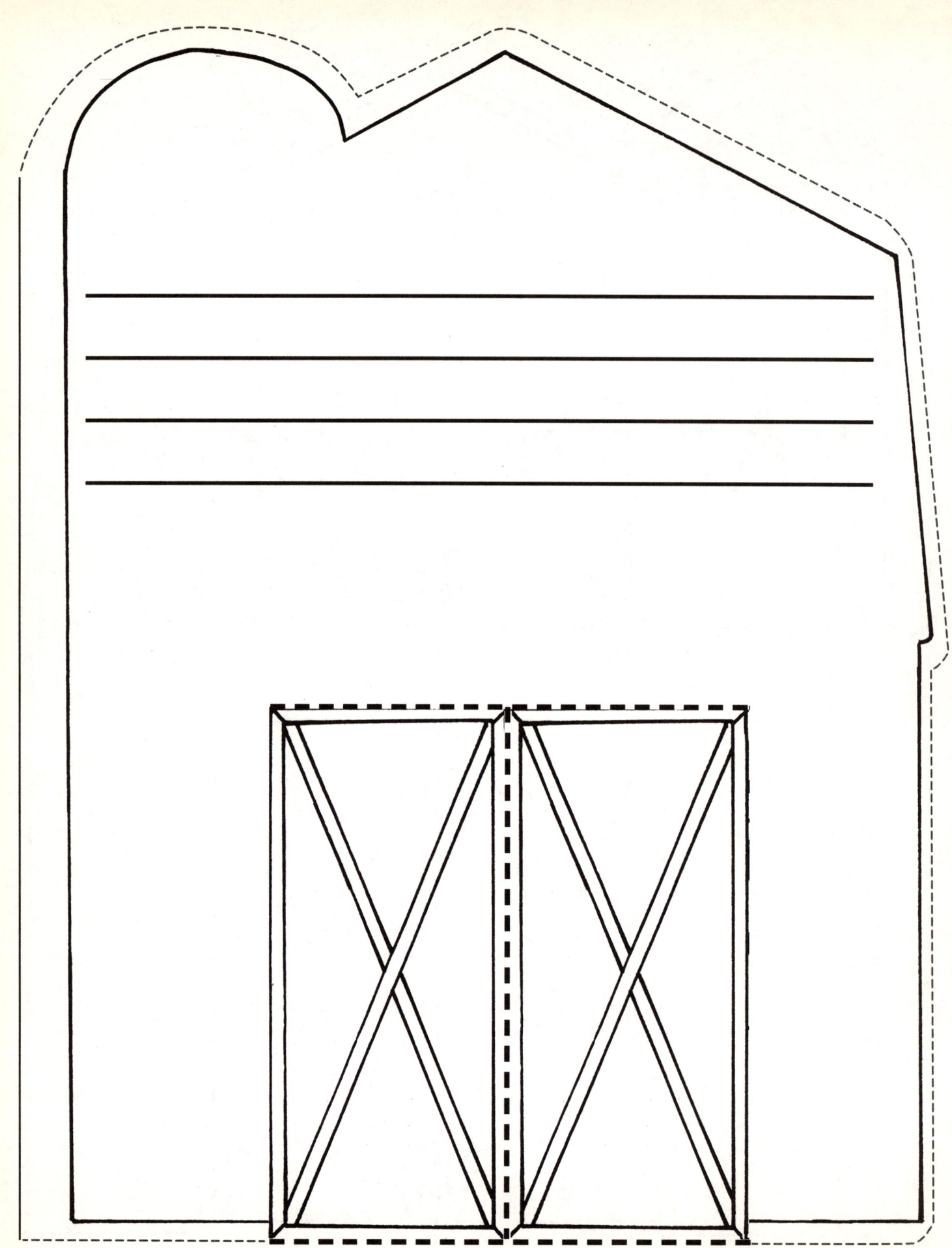

Barn Dance

25 Fun-Filled Collaborative Books Based on Favorite Picture Books

# The Biggest Pumpkin Ever

• • • • • • • **by Steven Kroll (Holiday House, 1984)**

Invite students to come up with their own creative solutions to the problem in the story. How will two mice move their enormous pumpkin into town for the contest?

**Themes:** Autumn, Halloween, Cooperation, Plants, Life Cycles

## Cover Preparation Idea

1. To make front and back covers, trace the cover template twice onto sturdy orange paper. Cut out the shapes.
2. Write the title "Solving a Pumpkin Problem."
3. To make a jack-o'-lantern face, cut eyes, nose, and mouth from black construction paper. Cut a stem from green paper. Glue them in place. Add any other details with thin black marker.

## Literature

Desmond and Clayton are two mice that grow an enormous pumpkin. They want to take their pumpkin to town for the pumpkin contest, but they do not know how to get it there. After reading the title, ask students to share what they know about pumpkins. Throughout the story, pause occasionally to ponder the predicament of these mice and talk about why their attempts did not work. What should they do next? As students offer ideas, briefly discuss the pros and cons of each. Continue and repeat as desired. Continue reading the story aloud until the sentence "Some were rolling them along the ground." Invite students to offer their own original solutions to Desmond and Clayton's dilemma.

## Writing & Art

Have a few volunteers share their ideas while you distribute the student writing pages. Instruct students to illustrate their solutions in the space provided. Then have students write their own brief endings based on the solution they illustrated. Provide writing guidance as necessary. Write the following prompt on the board: **"Desmond and Clayton can _____."** You might give children a word bank with words such as *pumpkin*, *contest*, *carve*, and *jack-o'-lantern*. After all students have completed and shared their story endings, finish reading Kroll's story aloud. Did anyone solve the problem as Kroll's mice did? Discuss that there is often more than one good solution to a problem.

## Beyond the Book

- Bring a variety of pumpkins to class and have students arrange them by size—smallest to largest, then largest to smallest.
- Read about the pumpkin life cycle, and create a sequential map showing how a pumpkin grows.

**Book Links:** *Apples and Pumpkins* by Anne Rockwell (Macmillan, 1989). A little girl visits a farm with her family to pick apples and pumpkins. Together, she and her mother carve the pumpkin into a jack-o'-lantern—just in time for Halloween!
*The Pumpkin Book* by Gail Gibbons (Holiday, 1999) chronicles the pumpkin's life cycle from seed to bud to plant to table through simple prose and detailed illustrations. ***Pumpkin, Pumpkin*** by Jeanne Titherington (Greenwillow Books, 1986). A boy follows the growth of his pumpkin seed through the spring, the summer, and all the way into fall when it's ready to be picked and carved.

# Brown Bear, Brown Bear, What Do You See?

• • • • • • by Bill Martin, Jr. and Eric Carle (Holt, Rinehart, and Winston, 1967)

Children create their own version of this story by describing what a black cat might see on Halloween.

**Themes:** Farm, Animals, Fantasy

## Cover Preparation Idea

1. Photocopy the cover template onto gray paper. Mount it on sturdy paper and cut out the shape. To make the back cover, trace onto sturdy paper and cut out. Draw a tail on the back cover.
2. Glue on large, movable eyes, if desired.
3. Draw fur and any additional details with a black crayon.

## Literature

The question "What do you see?" is answered throughout the book by various animals in a repetitive pattern. Invite students to join as you read each question, and encourage children to predict what each animal will see next. Read the book again, this time inviting students to read along as they use the illustrations to guide their recollection of the text.

## Writing & Art

Explain that children will create their own story about the things that a black cat might see on Halloween. On the board, write the prompt: **"I see a _____ _____ staring at me."** Remind students to fill in both the color of the object and the object, such as "green witch" or "orange jack-o'-lantern." Distribute the student writing pages. Explain that students will write their response on the lines and draw an illustration in the space. Provide writing assistance as necessary. When students have finished, bind the pages together and read the collaborative book aloud. As you are reading, add questions to replicate the pattern in the book—for example, "Black cat, black cat, what do you see?"

## Beyond the Book

- Read nonfiction books about bears. Compare and contrast the various kinds of bears and their behaviors, including diets and habitats. Organize and graph bear facts.

- Discuss various Halloween traditions. Allow students to share their Halloween experiences with the class.

- Divide a bulletin board into sections, one for each color. Have students illustrate or cut pictures from magazines and display them in the appropriate section by color.

**Book Links:** *Angelina's Halloween* by Katharine Holabird (Pleasant Company Publications, 2000). Angelina doesn't want her little sister to follow her on Halloween! The detailed illustrations include many things one might see on Halloween. *Growl! A Book About Bears* by Melvin Berger (Cartwheel Books, 1999) provides a more in-depth look at how bears live and includes color photographs. *Polar Bear, Polar Bear, What Do You Hear?* by Bill Martin, Jr. (Henry Holt & Company, 1991) has the same premise as the book for this activity, but this time the question is "What do you hear?"

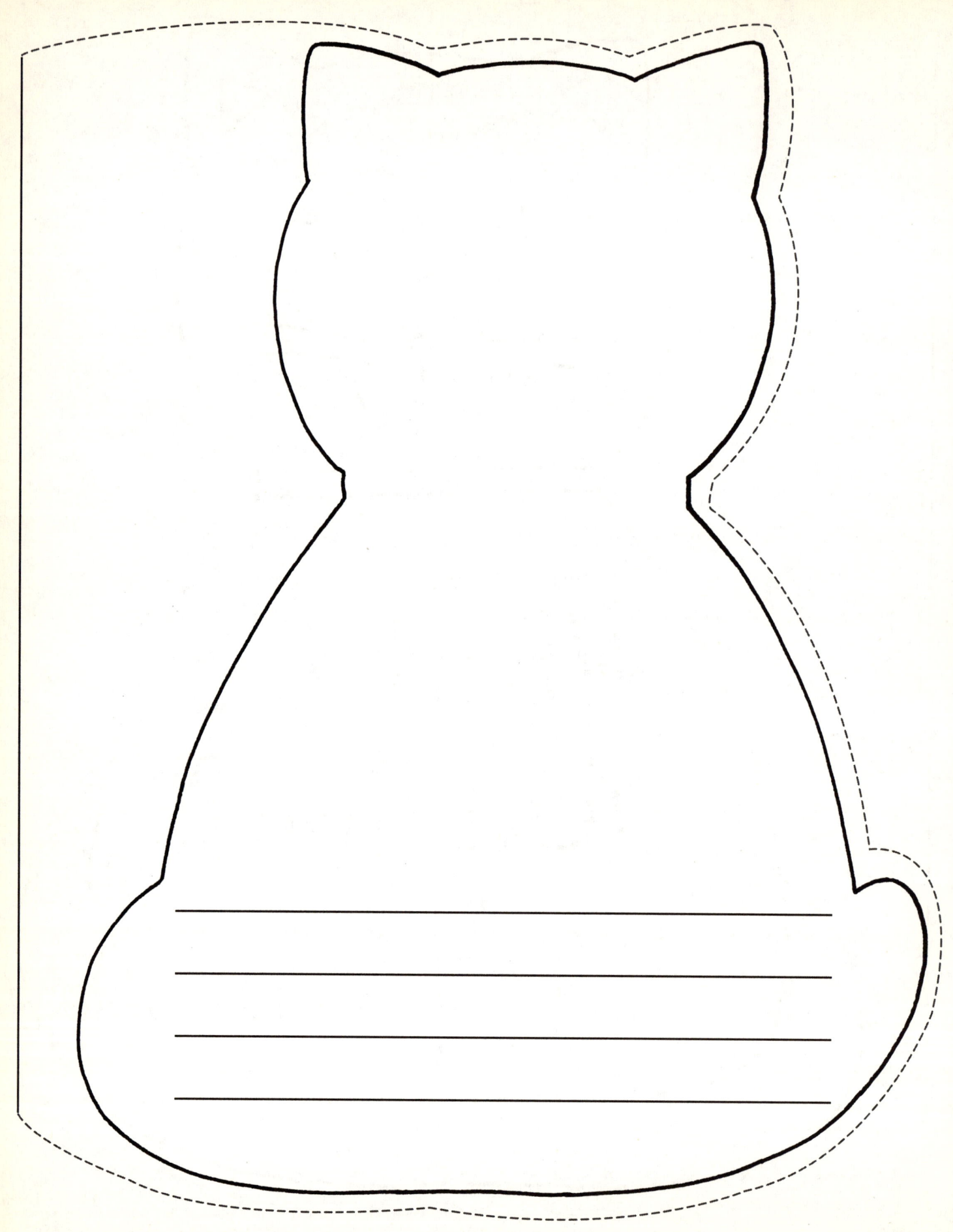

34  Brown Bear, Brown Bear, What Do You See?    25 Fun-Filled Collaborative Books Based on Favorite Picture Books

# In 1492

### by Jean Marzollo (Scholastic, 1991)

The year is 1492 and what does Columbus do? Invite students along on Columbus's famous journey.

**Themes:** Columbus Day, Early Explorers

## Cover Preparation Idea

1. Photocopy the cover template onto white paper. Mount it on sturdy paper and cut out. For the back cover, trace onto sturdy paper and cut out.
2. Draw people on the ship.

## Literature

In this story, Christopher Columbus's first voyage to North America is described through rhyme. In the author's introduction, readers are briefly introduced to Queen Isabella and her rationale for supporting Columbus's journey. Before reading, make a K-W-L chart on easel paper or the chalkboard (What I Know, What I Want to Know, What I Learned). List things your class already knows about Columbus and things they want to know. After the story, fill in the last column with newly learned information.

## Writing & Art

After discussing how Columbus may have prepared for his trip, invite students to pretend that they will be traveling with Columbus on his great voyage. Students may choose to write about the items that they would take on a trip with Columbus, or how they would feel about leaving their homes and families. Students may also choose to write a letter to Queen Isabella to persuade her to support Columbus's voyage. Have children draw a picture to illustrate their writing.

### Beyond the Book

- Using a large map, chart Columbus's journey.
- Study the evolution of ships—from sails to engines. Discuss with students which type of ship they think is easier to sail.

**Book Links: *Christopher Columbus*** by Stephen Krensky (Random House, 1991) is an easy-to-understand account of the milestones in Columbus's life. ***Where Do You Think You're Going, Christopher Columbus?*** by Jean Fritz (Putnam, 1980) offers a comprehensive account of Columbus's life and travels for more advanced readers. ***Young Christopher Columbus, Discoverer of New Worlds*** by Eric Carpenter (Troll Associates, 1992) tells Columbus's story for very young readers.

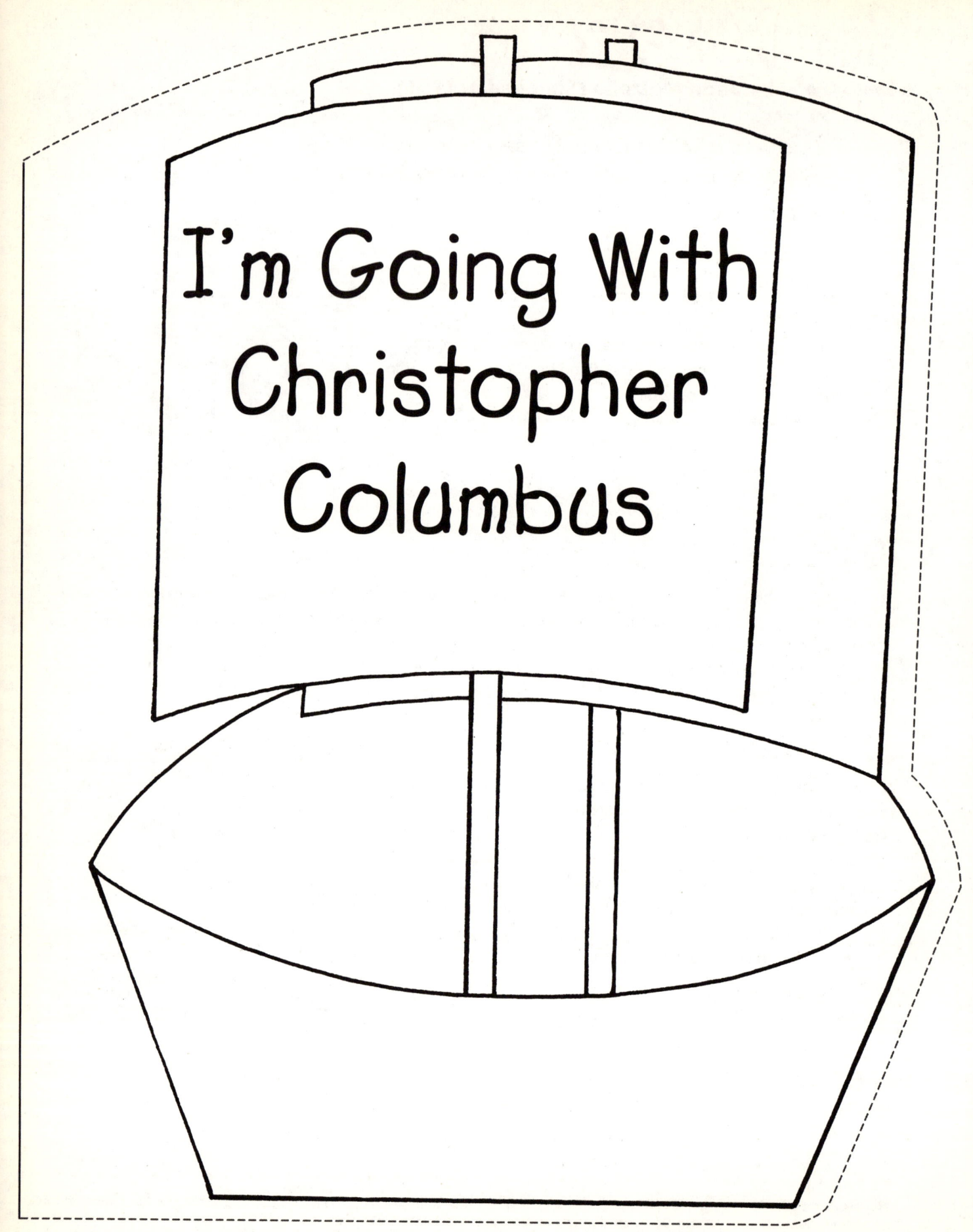

# Pigs Will Be Pigs

**by Amy Axelrod (Four Winds Press, 1994)**

After they read about the Pig family's feast, students write what they like to pig out on.

**Themes:** Money, Pigs, Food

## Cover Preparation Idea

1. Trace the cover template onto sturdy pink paper and cut out. For the back cover, trace onto sturdy paper and cut out.
2. Cut the nose, face, and ear shapes from pink paper.
3. Fold the ears accordion style to give them a three-dimensional quality.
4. Trace the face and nose onto cardboard and cut out the shapes.
5. Glue the paper shapes on top of the cardboard shapes. Before the glue dries, insert the ears between the paper and cardboard at the top of the face.
6. Glue the nose onto the face and glue the face onto the body.
7. Use a black marker to accentuate any details and write the title "Pig Out!"
8. Wrap a white or pink pipe cleaner around a pencil to give it a curly shape. Then glue or tape the pipe cleaner to the inside back cover so that it sticks out.

## Literature

The Pig family wants a snack, but there's no food in their refrigerato[r]. Together, they search the house for change and round up enough [to go to a] restaurant. Before you begin, ask students what they know about pigs [and dis-]cuss its origin.

## Writing & Art

Write the following prompt on the board: **"I like to pig out on _____**" pages and have children respond to the prompt. Encourage more details, such as why they like the food they chose. Ask: "What does it like to eat or drink with it?" Invite children to add an illustration.

## Beyond the Book

- Write a lunch menu of foods and their prices. Divide the class into groups, and give each group a bucket of play coins. Have each group decide what they will order and then determine how much it will cost. Do they have enough?

- Create a chart with a column each for pennies, nickels, dimes, quarters, and the various bills that appear in the story. Reread the story. Have volunteers fill in the chart as each coin or bill is found.

**Book Links:** *If You Give a Pig a Pancake* by Laura Numeroff (Laura Geringer, 1998). Follow the adventures of one very energetic piglet full circle, as the story ends where it begins! *Pigs* by Gail Gibbons (Holiday, 1999) provides a comprehensive look at pigs—life cycle, behavior, physical characteristics, breeds, and so on. *Pigs Aplenty, Pigs Galore* by David McPhail (Dutton, 1993). What happens when partying pigs invade your home?

# "What's in the Sack?" From Where the Sidewalk Ends

### by Shel Silverstein (Harper and Row, 1974)

The pages in this collaborative book are brown paper bags! Kids write a riddle and draw the answer beneath the flap.

**Themes:** Riddles, Poetry

## Cover Preparation Idea

1. You will need two brown grocery bags (approximately 8 by 12 inches) for the front and back covers and an additional bag of the same size for each student. Keep the bags flat.
2. For the front cover, position a bag horizontally so that the opening is on the left and the bottom flap is facing up. Draw a child holding a sack, and paste it onto the flap.
3. Write the title "What's in the Sack?" to the left of the flap.

## Literature

In this humorous poem, a man is continually asked about the contents of his sack. After discussing the poem, show students a paper bag in which you have stored an object. Invite children to guess what's in the bag as you provide clues.

## Writing & Art

In advance, cut lined paper into rectangles that will fit on the bottom flap of the bags. (Reproducible lined paper appears on page 7.) Distribute the paper sacks and lined paper rectangles. Have students write: "What's in my sack?" in pencil on the left side of the bag and then trace with marker or crayon. Invite students to think of an object that they could hide in a sack. Have students lift the flap and draw a picture of the object they chose. Next, have students write clues on the lined paper. Provide guidance as necessary. When writing is complete, glue the clue sheets on the flap.

## Beyond the Book

- Place a mystery object in a box and play 20 questions. Have students ask yes or no questions about the object, such as "Is it hard?" or "Is it a toy?" until they have enough information to guess the object.

- Each day, display a riddle and encourage students to place responses in an answer box. At the end of the day, draw a response from the box. Read the responses aloud and continue choosing responses until one is correct. Have the winner explain the solution to the class.

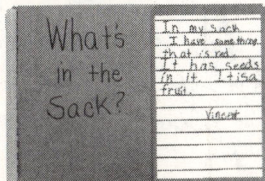

Inside Page

Inside Page, Flap Open

**Book Links:** *Biggest Riddle Book in the World* by Joesph Rosenbloom (Sterling, 1976) is a collection of riddles that are sure to stump! *My First Riddles* by Judith Hoffman Corwin (HarperFestival, 1998). Traditional yet simple riddles are presented. Rhyming questions reveal answers on the following page. *Riddles and More Riddles!* by Bennett Cerf (Random House, 1999) contains simple riddles that beginning readers will enjoy.

# Sadie and the Snowman

•••••••• by Allen Morgan (Kids Can Press, 1985)

After reading about Sadie's snowman, children write simple snowman poems.

**Themes:** Snow, Adjectives, Poetry

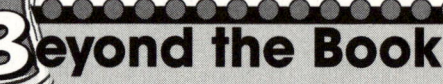

## Cover Preparation Idea

1. To make front and back covers, trace the cover template twice onto sturdy white paper. Cut out the shapes.
2. Using felt, fabric, feathers, buttons, and cut paper, "dress" the snowman. Glue on eyes, nose, mouth, hat, scarf, buttons, and anything else you'd like.
3. Write the title "Our Snowmen" in the center of the body.

## Literature

Sadie manages to make her snowman last a long time. Each time he melts, Sadie uses ingenuity to preserve him until the next snow. When Sadie's snowman melts the first time, pause and ask children to predict what will happen next. As you read, pause to discuss how Sadie's ideas are effective. Why doesn't the snowman melt away?

## Writing & Art

Begin with a discussion about adjectives: What are they and how do we use them? Ask children, "What are some other words we could use to describe Sadie's snowman?" On chart paper, make a circle map of adjectives that describe a snowman. Add students' suggestions to the chart. Distribute the student writing pages and have children write "Snowman" on the first and last lines. Students then choose five different adjectives from the chart and write them on the remaining lines.

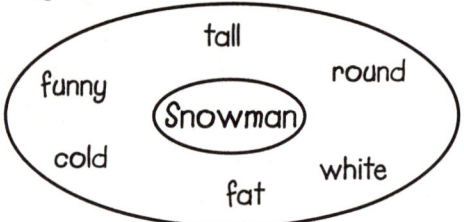

Provide students with crayons, markers, glue, colored paper, and felt with which to decorate their snowmen.

## Beyond the Book

- How is snow made? Read about the formation of snow crystals and make your own snowflakes out of paper.
- Explore other forms of poetry such as limericks. Have students create wintry acrostics, using words such as *snow, ice,* and *January.*

**Book Links:** *Many Luscious Lollipops: A Book About Adjectives* by Ruth Heller (Grosset & Dunlap, 1989). This rhyming narrative tells all there is to know about adjectives. *Once Upon Ice and Other Frozen Poems* selected by Jane Yolen (Boyds Mills, 1997). Compelling photos of natural ice are described in verse. *Snowballs* by Lois Ehlert (Harcourt Brace, 1995). Visit with snow people made from various untraditional materials.

# Dear Tooth Fairy

**by Kath Mellentin and Tim Wood (Little Simon, 1997)**

Invite children to learn about dental care while reading about this magical nighttime visitor!

**Themes:** Teeth, Fantasy, Dental Health Month (February)

## Cover Preparation Idea

1. To make front and back covers, trace the cover template twice onto sturdy white paper. Cut out the shapes.
2. Using a marker, write the title "The Tooth Fairy."
3. Draw a picture of the tooth fairy with teeth around her. Use silver glitter, glitter spray, or sparkle paint to decorate the teeth.

## Literature

Where does the tooth fairy come from? And how did she get her remarkable job? Invite students to share what they "know" about the tooth fairy. Write their ideas on the board or on chart paper. Explain that you're going to read a book that describes what the authors think is true about the tooth fairy. After reading aloud the story, invite children to give their responses.

## Writing & Art

Remind students that no one's really sure how the tooth fairy got her job, exactly what she does, or exactly how she does it. Let them know that this should not keep them from coming up with their own ideas about her. Remind students that they've just heard some ideas about how the tooth fairy got her job; now, you'd like them to speculate about the particulars of her job. Write on the board or chart paper: **"I think the tooth fairy_____."** Invite students to share their ideas about what the tooth fairy does with the teeth she collects. Then have each child write his or her idea on the student writing pages and then draw an illustration supporting the text.

## Beyond the Book

- Invite a local dentist to speak to your class about dental health.

- Discuss foods that are good for teeth and foods that are not. Have students cut from magazines pictures of smart food choices and poor food choices. Display on a bulletin board.

- Who's lost a tooth in your class? Who's lost more than one? Who has loose teeth? Count the total number of loose teeth and lost teeth. As a class, create a graph of the information you've collected. Cut teeth from construction paper to represent each loose or lost tooth and tape them to the graph. Post the graph in a prominent place in the classroom and update as needed.

**Book Links:** *Food for Healthy Teeth* by Helen Frost (Pebble Books, 1999). Find out how what you eat affects your teeth. *The Real Tooth Fairy* by Marilyn Kaye (Harcourt, 1990). A mother's ingenious reasoning explains her uncanny resemblance to the tooth fairy. *Tooth Fairy* by Audrey Wood (Child's Play International, 1989). Find out who gets the last laugh when a little girl tries to trick the tooth fairy.

# The Tooth Fairy

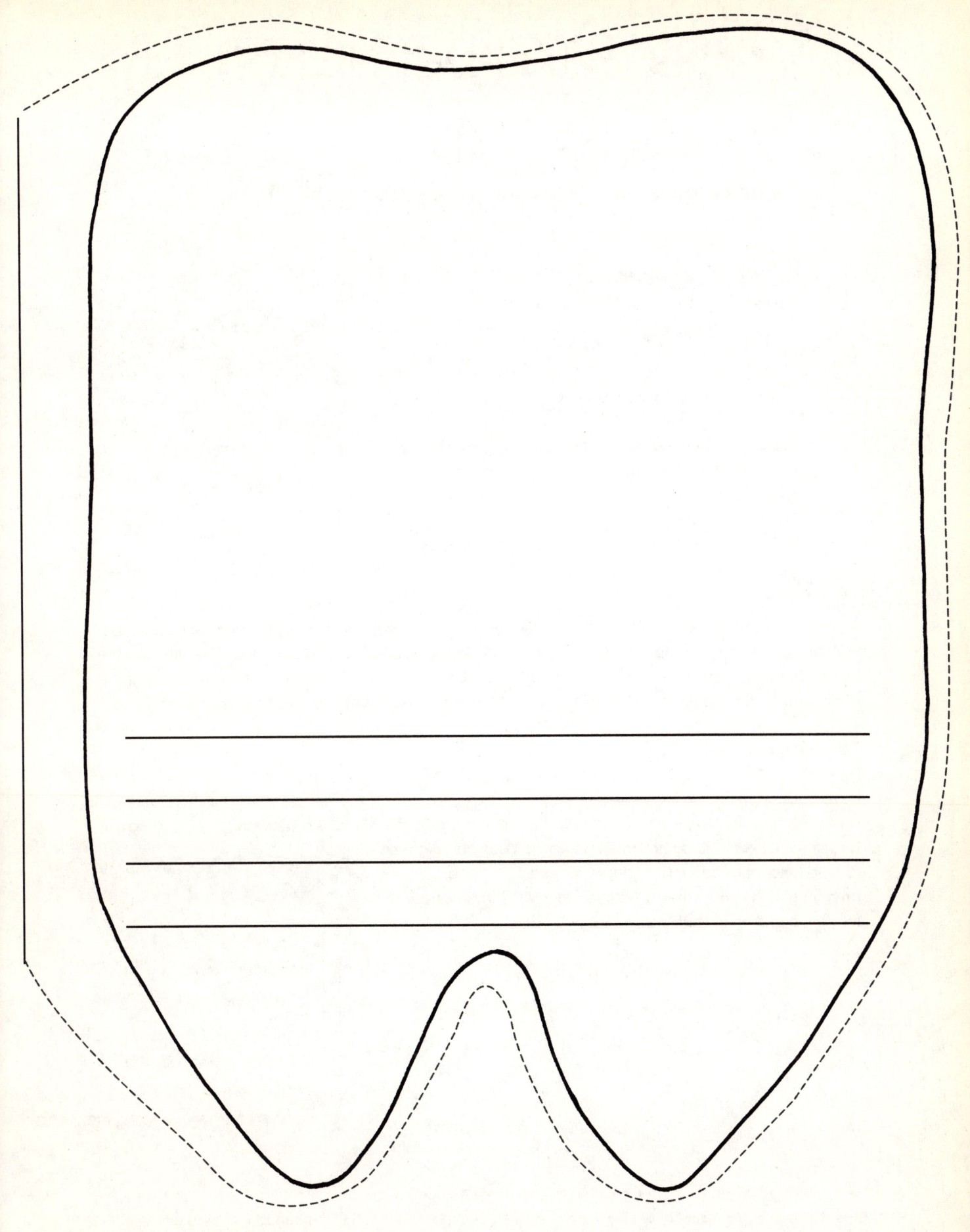

# If the Dinosaurs Came Back

••••• **by Bernard Most (Harcourt Brace Jovanovich, 1978)**

Children consider how dinosaurs might come in handy in today's world.

**Themes:** Dinosaurs, Fantasy

## Cover Preparation Idea

1. Photocopy the cover template. Mount it on sturdy paper and cut out. For the back cover, trace onto sturdy paper and cut out.
2. Color the cover as desired.
3. Glue plastic grass or green foam peanuts along the bottom.

## Literature

A young boy imagines a world in which dinosaurs and people live in harmony, where dinosaurs use their strength and size to help people and make the world a better place. Before you begin, read the title and ask children to predict what they think the story might be about. As you read, elicit discussion. At the conclusion of the story, take a class vote: Who would like to see the dinosaurs come back?

## Writing & Art

Have students reflect on the ways a dinosaur could make each of their lives a little bit better. Pass out the student writing sheets. On the board, write the following prompt: **"If I had a dinosaur, _____."** Have students write a sentence or two about how a dinosaur might be able to help them do certain things—for example, reach objects on high shelves. When they have finished writing, invite students to draw a picture to illustrate their ideas.

### Beyond the Book

- Research different types of dinosaurs using the Internet, encyclopedias, and books.
- Have a class dinosaur exhibit. Draw or model dinosaurs and label body parts.

**Book Links:** *An Alphabet of Dinosaurs* by Peter Dodson (Scholastic, 1995). This beautifully illustrated text offers brief, informative descriptions of 26 dinosaurs, one for each letter of the alphabet. *Dinosaur Bones* by Aliki (Crowell, 1988). Find out how scientists use fossils to prove the existence of dinosaurs. *What Happened to the Dinosaurs?* by Franklin Mansfield Branley (Crowell, 1989) explores what scientists think happened to the dinosaurs. Illustrated by Caldecott-winner Marc Simont.

# Dinosaur Helpers

25 Fun-Filled Collaborative Books Based on Favorite Picture Books — If the Dinosaurs Came Back

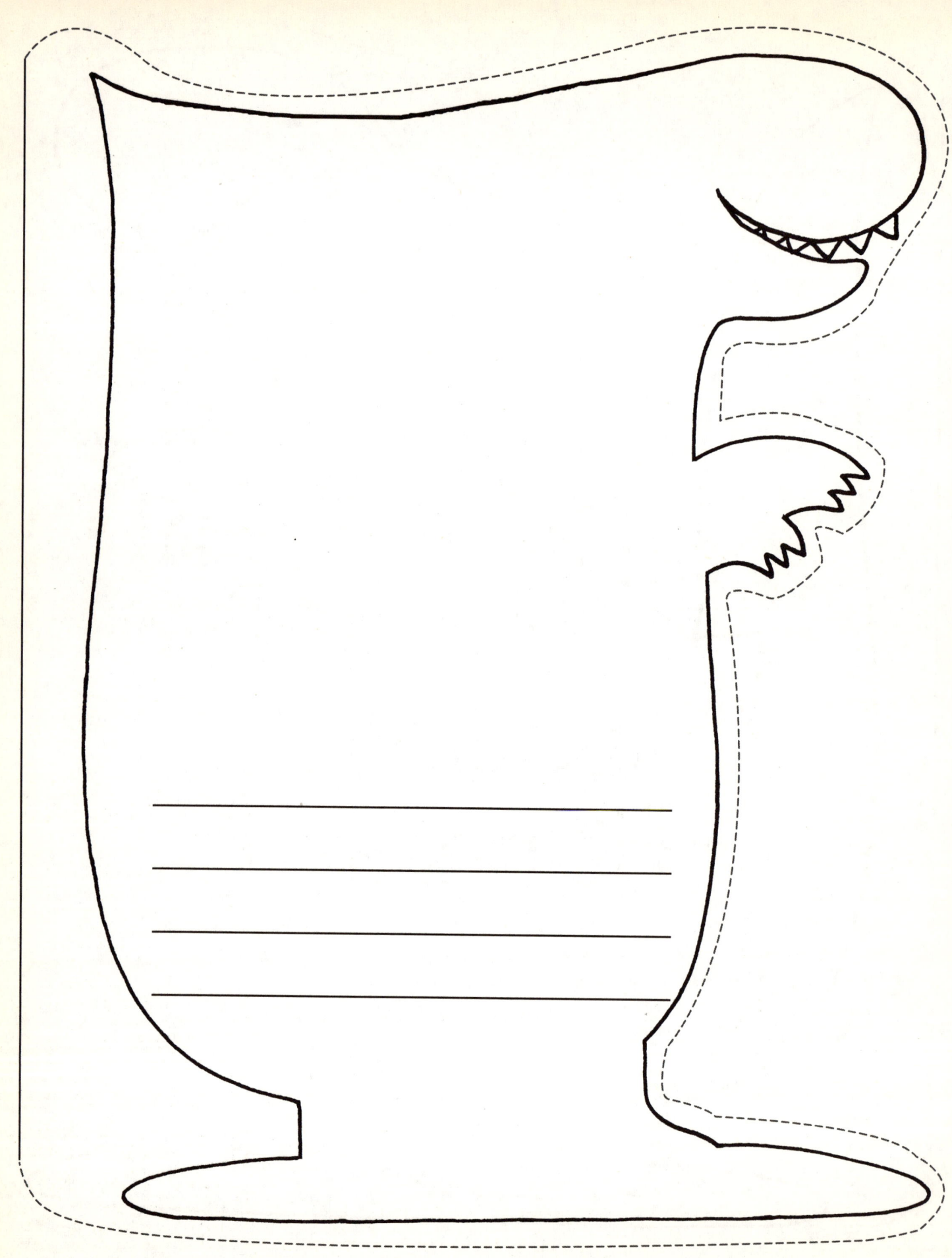

50 *If the Dinosaurs Came Back* — 25 Fun-Filled Collaborative Books Based on Favorite Picture Books

# The Grouchy Ladybug

• • • • • • **by Eric Carle (T. Y. Crowell, 1977)**

Children write about what makes them grouchy.

**Themes:** Ladybugs, Feelings

## Cover Preparation Idea

1. To make front and back covers, trace the cover template twice onto sturdy red paper. Cut out the shapes.
2. Write the title "What Bugs Me," using black marker.
3. Add black circle stickers or draw black dots. Attach movable eyes or draw eyes. Draw a frowning mouth to make the ladybug look grouchy.
4. Punch three holes along the bottom edge. Bend a small strip of black pipe cleaner through each hole to create two legs. Twist each set of legs together at the top and then bend the bottoms into feet. For antennae, curl smaller strips of pipe cleaners and attach to the head with glue.

## Literature

An ill-tempered ladybug learns that to have friends, she needs to be a friend. Discuss what it means to be grouchy. Can students give examples of when they've had a grouchy day? How do they think others feel when they act grouchy? Read the title and have students make predictions about the story. Throughout the story, whenever a character acts grouchy, stop reading and ask students to imagine how the other characters feel as a result. At the end, discuss what the ladybug learned.

## Writing & Art

What does it mean to "bug" someone? Ask children what this expression means, and explain the play on words. Ask students to describe things that bug them. Pass out the student writing sheets. Write the following prompt on the board: **"What bugs me is _____."** Have students write a sentence or two about something that bugs them and why.

## Beyond the Book

- Explore emotional responses. How do students act when they're feeling happy? Sad? Frightened? Lonely? Have students make faces to reflect different moods.

- Launch a mini-unit on ladybugs. Read nonfiction books that describe the ladybug's life cycle, eating habits, and so on.

- Compare and contrast ladybugs to other insects, using a Venn diagram.

**Book Links:** *Are You a Ladybug?* by Brian and Jill Cutting (Kingfisher, 2000). This beautifully illustrated work allows the reader to "grow up" as a ladybug. *The Grumpy Morning* by Pamela Duncan Edwards (Hyperion, 1998). When the farmer oversleeps, her impatient farm animals become grumpy. *How Are You Peeling? Foods With Moods* by Saxton Freymann and Joost Elffers (Arthur Levine, 1999). The authors transform ordinary fruits and vegetables into characters whose emotions run the gamut. *The Ultimate Bug Book* by Luise Woelflein (Western, 1993) compares ladybugs with their other insect relatives in a uniquely designed book.

52 The Grouchy Ladybug · 25 Fun-Filled Collaborative Books Based on Favorite Picture Books

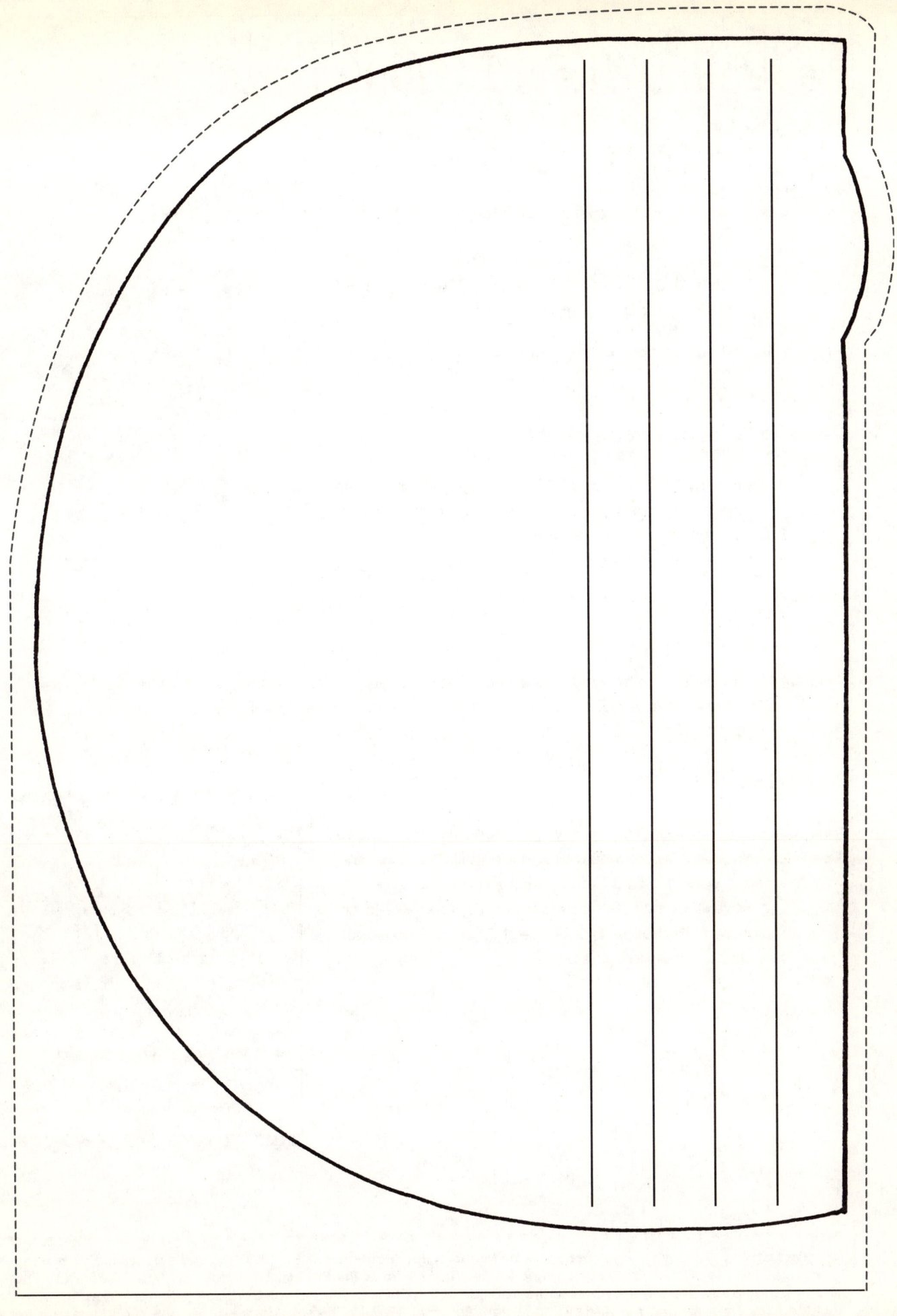

25 Fun-Filled Collaborative Books Based on Favorite Picture Books          The Grouchy Ladybug  53

# Shibumi and the Kitemaker

### by Mercer Mayer (Marshall Cavendish, 1999)

Inspired by this original fairy tale, children write about their own magic kite.

**Themes:** Kites, Japanese Culture, Fantasy

## Cover Preparation Idea

1. Photocopy the cover template. Mount it on sturdy paper and cut out. For the back cover, trace onto sturdy paper and cut out.
2. Color the kite and background.
3. Glue yarn for the string and cotton balls for the clouds.

## Literature

Shibumi wants to change her world—and she takes some very drastic steps to do so. While reading, ask students to describe things about the world that they'd like to change. Are Shibumi's concern's valid? Ask children what they would have done in her situation. Do they feel Shibumi's solution is reasonable?

## Writing & Art

In this tale, Shibumi leaves her family's kingdom and finds solace on a faraway coast. Where would your students like to travel to? On the board, write **"I would like to ride my magic kite to _____."** Have students write about where they would like to go and then draw an illustration. Encourage children to write about what they would see or do in this place.

## Beyond the Book

- Imagine what Earth would look like from a kite's point of view high in the sky. Have students draw their representations, and display them around the classroom.

- Make your own kites and hold a kite festival outside to give children a chance to fly them.

**Book Links:** *Curious George Flies a Kite* by Margaret Rey (Houghton Mifflin, 1958). In trouble again, the curious monkey's adventures this time involve a kite. *Kites: Magic Wishes That Fly Up to the Sky* by Demi (Crown, 1999) is a beautifully illustrated tale of a magic kite and the story behind the tradition of the Chinese kite festival. Complete kite-making instructions are included. *The Emperor and the Kite* by Jane Yolen (Philomel, 1967). In this Caldecott Honor book, a princess uses her kite to save the day.

56 Shibumi and the Kitemaker  25 Fun-Filled Collaborative Books Based on Favorite Picture Books

# Rechenka's Eggs

### by Patricia Polacco (Philomel, 1988)

Celebrate spring—or any season—with an activity inspired by Ukrainian egg decoration.

**Themes:** Russian Folklore, Spring Festivals, Ukrainian Crafts

## Cover Preparation Idea

1. To make front and back covers, trace the cover template twice onto sturdy light-colored paper. Cut out the shapes.
2. Decorate the egg as desired, using materials such as stickers, rickrack, markers, and paint.
3. Write the title "Our Eggs."

## Literature

While Old Babushka is decorating her eggs for the festival, she comes upon an injured goose and cares for it. What happens when the goose breaks all of Babushka's carefully painted eggs?

## Writing & Art

In advance, photocopy and cut out the student writing pages. Photocopy the cover template so that there is one for each child. Cut out the egg template and then cut each egg in half, just below the title. Place the bottom half of the egg on top of each student writing page so that it covers up the writing lines. Glue or staple along the left edges.

Invite students to look back at the book illustrations for inspiration. Then have them decorate their eggs. Supply as many materials as desired: crayons, markers, sequins, stickers, and so on. When children have finished decorating, encourage them to write a detailed description of their egg on the lines.

### Beyond the Book

- Decorate hard-boiled eggs. Draw designs on each egg, pressing lightly with crayon, to resemble the Russian designs. Dip into egg dye and allow to dry. Using a thin brush, apply tempera paints in simple line or dot patterns.

- Plan a study about animals that lay eggs. Read and discuss *Chickens Aren't the Only Ones* by Ruth Heller (Grosset & Dunlap, 1981).

**Book Links:** *The Talking Eggs* by Robert D. San Souci (Dial, 1989) is an American folktale about some very special eggs. *The Easter Egg Artists* by Adrienne Adams (Scribner, 1976). Orson grows into his own style as he learns to decorate more than just eggs. *Spring: An Alphabet Acrostic* by Steven Schnur (Clarion Books, 1999) is an acrostic book all about spring.

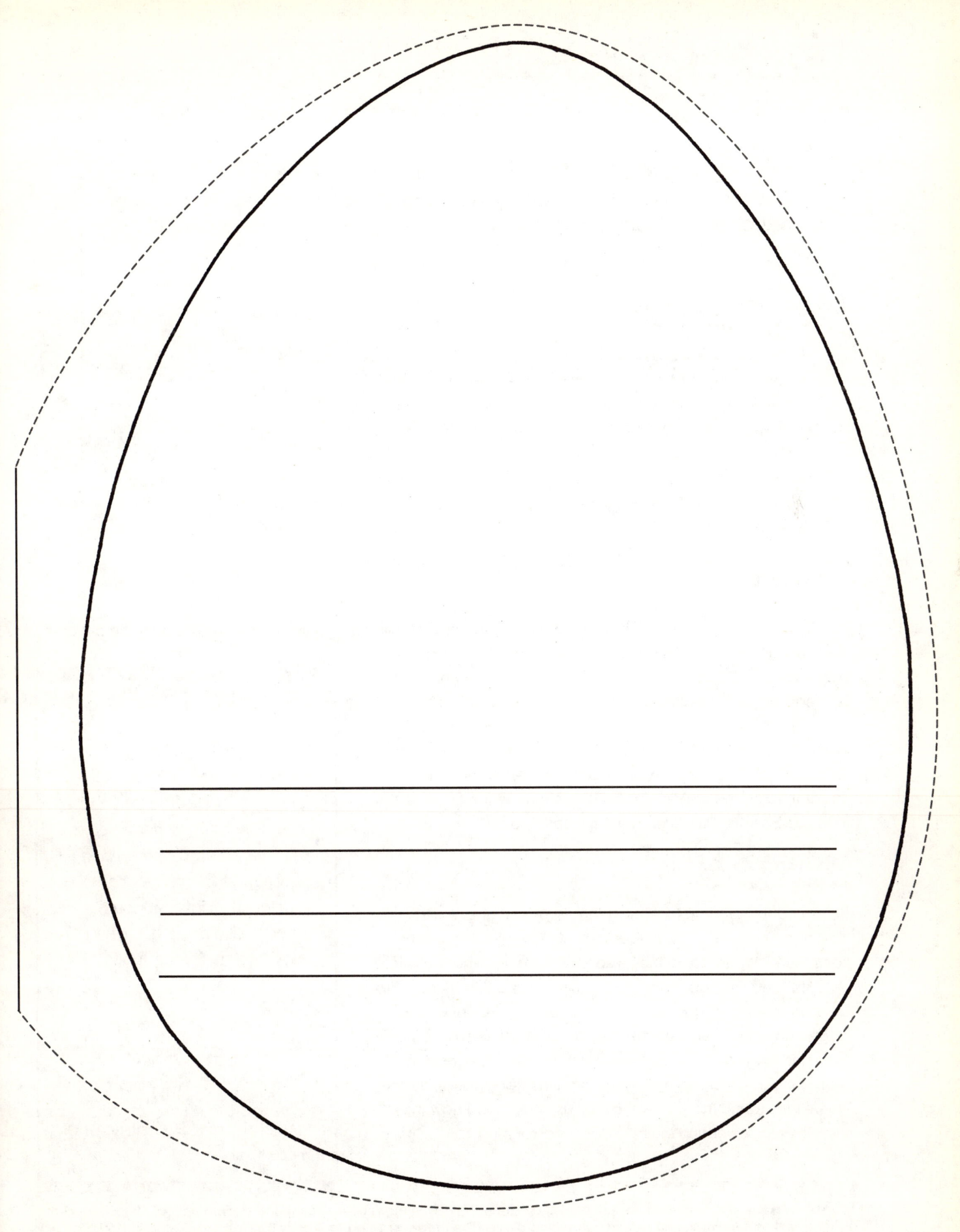

# Goggles!

### by Ezra Jack Keats (Macmillan, 1969)

What treasures might you uncover in someone else's junk? Join Peter and his friends as they defend their newly prized possession, a pair of discarded motorcycle goggles that they found in a pile of trash.

**Themes:** Urban Communities, Bully Prevention, Author Study (Keats)

## Cover Preparation Idea

1. Photocopy the cover template several times onto construction paper. Cut out the goggles so that you have three for the cover and one for each student. If desired, cut out the eyeholes and glue small pieces of cellophane behind each for lenses.
2. To make the front cover, decorate three pairs of goggles and glue them onto a sturdy sheet of colored paper.
3. Write the title "Our Goggles."
4. Use a plain sheet of sturdy paper for the back cover.

## Literature

This Caldecott Honor book vividly portrays an urban community. Use this story to begin or conclude a class study on communities. Before you begin, remind students that Peter lives in a city. List characteristics of urban communities on chart paper. Then list the characteristics of your school's surrounding neighborhood on another sheet. As you read, pause to discuss the similarities and differences between Peter's environment and that of your students'. When Peter feels threatened by the bullies, discuss his options. When finished, take a class vote: Did Peter make a smart choice?

## Writing & Art

Have students pretend that they found a pair of goggles in a garbage heap. What might they look like? Would they want to keep them? When would they wear them and for what purpose? Give students the paper goggles along with markers, glitter, and other supplies to decorate them. Distribute the student writing pages. Have children glue the goggles onto the center of the face and draw a picture of themselves wearing the goggles. Then encourage children to write about their goggles, including where they found them, how they will use them, and how they think they look wearing their newest accessory.

## Beyond the Book

- Read stories rich with the urban experience and non-fictional accounts of urban life; discuss the similarities and differences between urban environments and your own community. Have students create dioramas depicting daily life in various types of communities.

- Talk frankly with students about bullying. Read stories in which characters are bullied; How do the characters handle the situation? Is their solution reasonable?

**Book Links:** *Apt. 3* by Ezra Jack Keats (Macmillan, 1971). Two young boys explore the environment of their apartment building while searching for an elusive harmonica player. *The Meanest Thing to Say* by Bill Cosby (Scholastic, 1997). The new kid won't bully Little Bill and his friends for long! *Under New York* by Linda Oatman High (Holiday House, 2001) vividly portrays urban energy as readers are treated to beautifully illustrated vignettes of above- and below-ground activities.

# Hide and Snake
by Keith Baker (Harcourt Brace Jovanovich, 1991)

After challenging children to find snakes in hidden pictures, invite children to create their own pictures with hidden surprises!

**Themes:** Snakes, Pets

## Cover Preparation Idea

1. Photocopy the cover template. Mount it on sturdy paper and cut out. For the back cover, trace onto sturdy paper and cut out.
2. Color the snake using brightly colored markers.
3. Add a movable eye; attach bits of aluminum foil or iridescent cellophane for scales, if desired.

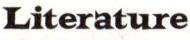

## Literature

This is a story about a clever snake that hides among familiar objects. As you read, leave ample time for students to study the picture and find the snake. Encourage students to give their classmates a chance to find the snake before revealing its hiding place. If necessary, repeat the rhyming clues as you slowly sweep the book past your audience. When you've finished reading, ask students whether they think the events in this story could actually take place. Ask students to describe how a real snake might look, what it might eat, and where it might live and hide.

## Writing & Art

Distribute the student writing pages. Challenge students to draw a scene that includes a camouflaged snake somewhere within it. Allow ample time for children to create these illustrations. When students have finished, give each student a paper strip that covers the bottom portion of the page (approximately 3 inches tall and 7 inches wide). On this strip, have students write: "Can you find (student's name) snake?" Help kids place the strip on top of the writing lines. Then paste along the left edge so that it creates a flap. Underneath, have students write the snake's location. When each student has finished and your book has been bound, gather for a round of Find the Snake!

## Beyond the Book

- Read informational books about snakes. Make and label snake diagrams.
- What kind of a pet does a snake make? Ask students how having a snake differs from having a dog, cat, or other pet. Are there any snake owners in your class?
- Study and create patterns. Why are patterns important? Examine the clever snake in the story. Can you find a pattern on its body?

**Book Links:** ***The Day Jimmy's Boa Ate the Wash*** by Trinka Hakes Noble (Dial, 1980). When Jimmy's unusual pet comes along on his class trip to the farm, hilarious situations ensue! ***Outside and Inside Snakes*** by Sandra Markle (Macmillan, 1995). This detailed work includes sharp, color photography, and an index/glossary. ***Slinky, Scaly Snakes*** by Jennifer Dussling (DK, 1998) allows beginning readers to access snake facts through fairly simple text and bright photos and illustrations. ***Verdi*** by Janell Cannon (Harcourt, 1997). A young snake learns that growing old isn't so bad, after all, in this exquisitely illustrated tale.

# Tar Beach

by Faith Ringgold (Crown, 1991)

After reading a magical story of a little girl's fantasy of flying, children write about their imaginative journey.

**Themes:** Summer, Fantasy, Quilting

## Cover Preparation Idea

1. Photocopy the cover template. Mount it on sturdy paper and cut out. For the back cover, trace onto sturdy paper and cut out.
2. Color the quilt squares on the border with a variety patterns, or cut wrapping paper squares of the same size and glue them onto the border.

## Literature

Faith Ringgold writes about her childhood memories of visiting Tar Beach, the rooftop escape during the summer in the city. Discuss why she called the roof "tar beach." Looking out at the lights of the city, she dreams of flying through the sky and seeing the city from a bird's-eye view. Explain that the illustrations in this story are part of a story quilt. Point out the quilted border on the cover and interior pages.

## Writing & Art

Ask children if they think this is a realistic story. What parts of the story could be real and what parts are purely fantasy? Tell children that they will write a fantasy book together, with each student contributing one page. Distribute student pages and invite students to think of a place that they would like to fly over. Then have them draw a picture of themselves flying over this place. Next, ask children to write about their drawings. If desired, write the following prompt on the board: **"I would fly to _____."** Encourage children to add any details they would like, such as why they chose this place, how it feels to fly, and what everything looks like from way up high. Finally, have children color the squares on the border or glue squares cut from wrapping paper.

## Beyond the Book

- Make collaborative class quilts from paper. Have each child contribute a square with art and writing. Determine in advance what the theme of the quilt will be (seasons, animals, all about me, and so on).

- Use quilts as an example of patterns. Look at quilts in books and magazines and challenge children to determine the pattern. Provide squares of different colors and have children create their own quilt patterns. Have them ask classmates to describe the pattern.

**Book Links:** *The Keeping Quilt* by Patrica Polacco (Simon & Schuster, 1998) describes the many uses of a quilt as it is passed from one generation to the next. *The Patchwork Quilt* by Valerie Flournoy (Pearson Learning, 1985). When her grandmother becomes ill, Tanya finishes a quilt that holds meaning for their family. Illustrated by Jerry Pinkney. *The Quilt Story* by Tony Johnston, illustrated by Tomie dePaola (Putnam, 1985). Two girls from different times in history share the same quilt.

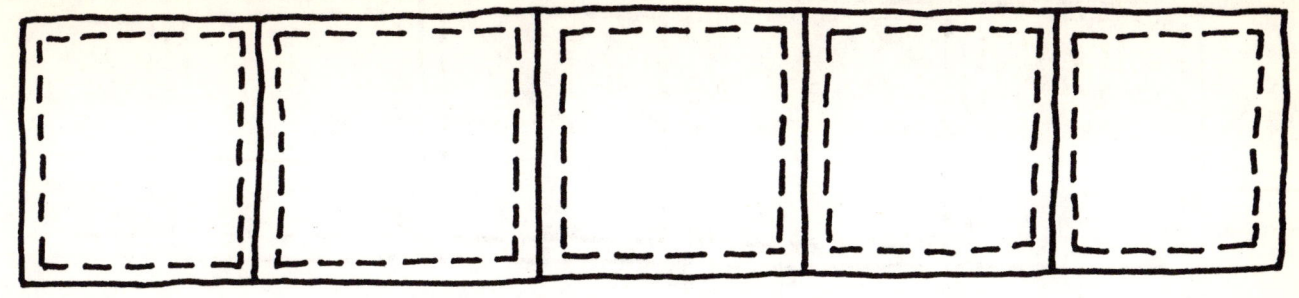

# Our Story Quilts

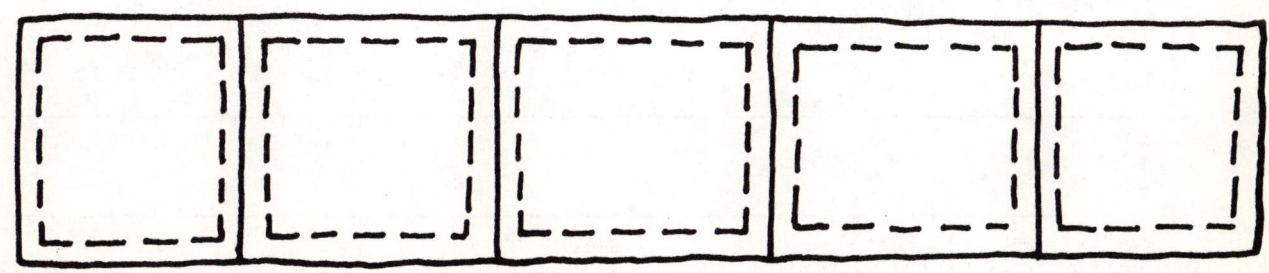

# Dear Zoo
## by Rod Campbell (Four Winds Press, 1982)

**W**hich animals at the zoo make good pets...and which animals do not?

**Themes:** Zoos, Animals, Pets

## Cover Preparation Idea

1. To make the front cover, photocopy the cover template and mount it on sturdy paper. Cut out the cover. For the back cover, trace onto sturdy paper and cut out.
2. Color the illustrations.

## Literature

In this story, a child writes to the zoo requesting a pet. Ask children to clarify why certain animals would not make good pets. For example, would it be difficult to keep a giraffe for a pet? Why? Encourage children to draw appropriate inferences, such as "A giraffe would be too tall to fit in my house."

## Writing & Art

Review the zoo animals that were mentioned in the story. Add other animals that children know live in a zoo. Write the following prompts on the board:

"A _____ would make a good pet because _____."

"A _____ would not make a good pet because _____."

Students can choose which prompt they would like to use and then draw an illustration to support their writing.

## Beyond the Book

- Arrange a class trip to a zoo—or you might take a virtual field trip instead! Visit the National Zoo Web site (http://natzoo.si.edu). You can read about the zoo, view photographs or a slide show, and watch live action on one of the zoo's several Web cams! Looking for more? Watch the video *The Big Zoo* (Little Mammoth Media, 1995).

- Read fiction and nonfiction about zoo animals. Make a chart with two columns, one labeled "Facts" and one labeled "Fantasy." Write information from the books in the appropriate columns.

**Book Links:** *Going to the Zoo* by Tom Paxton (Morrow, 1996). Rhyme, repetition, onomatopoeia, and action words make this trip to the zoo fun, fun, fun! *Good Night, Gorilla* by Peggy Rathmann (Putnam, 1994). A mischievous gorilla snatches the night watchman's key and unlocks the animals one by one. *If Anything Ever Goes Wrong at the Zoo* by Mary Jean Hendrick (Harcourt, 1993). When something goes wrong at the zoo, the zookeepers take Leslie up on her standing offer to watch over the animals—at her home. *Our Class Took a Trip to the Zoo* by Shirley Neitzel (Greenwillow, 2002). This simple, rhyming rebus chronicles one class's trip to the zoo. *Zoo* by Gail Gibbons (Crowell, 1987). Take a peek behind the scenes during a typical day at the zoo.

25 Fun-Filled Collaborative Books Based on Favorite Picture Books

Dear Zoo 71

# The Underwater Alphabet Book

### by Jerry Pallotta (Charlesbridge, 1991)

**K**ids discover a whole new underwater world and write about the sea creature they would most like to meet.

**Themes:** Ocean, Marine Life, Alphabet

## Cover Preparation Idea

1. Photocopy the cover template onto blue paper. Mount it on sturdy paper and cut out. For the back cover, trace onto sturdy paper and cut out.
2. Color the cover.
3. Using a thin marker, add details on the whale. If desired, add blue glitter spray, a movable eye, and aluminum foil or blue cellophane at the spout.

## Literature

This colorful ABC book introduces more than just letters. Before you begin, tell students that they are about to discover a whole new world! Invite them to guess where they will be going. Then explain that this journey will take place right here on Earth. After reading, have students recall the names of some underwater animals they studied. Show the Illustrations and give them the first letter of each name to help them remember, if necessary.

## Writing & Art

Have students imagine that they are going on an oceanic journey. What creature would they most like to meet and why? Have them draw the creature in its environment. Then invite students to write about what they drew, describing their creature and why they chose it. Give children the prompt: **"I would like to meet a _____ because _____."**

## Beyond the Book

- As a class, research endangered marine life such as coral reefs or manatees. Why are they endangered? What organizations help them? You might even organize a class fund-raiser and donate the proceeds to an organization you learned about during your research.

- Adopt a manatee at www.savethemanatee.org. Your class will receive a photo and profile of your newest class member.

- Create an underwater mural. Display it in the classroom or in the hallway.

**Book Links:** *A B Sea* by Bobbi Kalman (Crabtree, 1995). Striking photos and interesting facts leave readers wanting more in this original alphabet book. *Big Al* by Andrew Clements (Picture Book Studio, 1988). Big Al shows he can be a true friend in this oceanic spin on the classic lesson: Don't judge a book by its cover. *Rainbow Fish and the Big Blue Whale* by Marcus Pfister (North South Books, 1998). Rainbow Fish learns not to judge others solely by appearance. *What's Under the Ocean* by Janet Craig (Troll, 1982). Explore ocean life in this acclaimed science series for beginning readers.

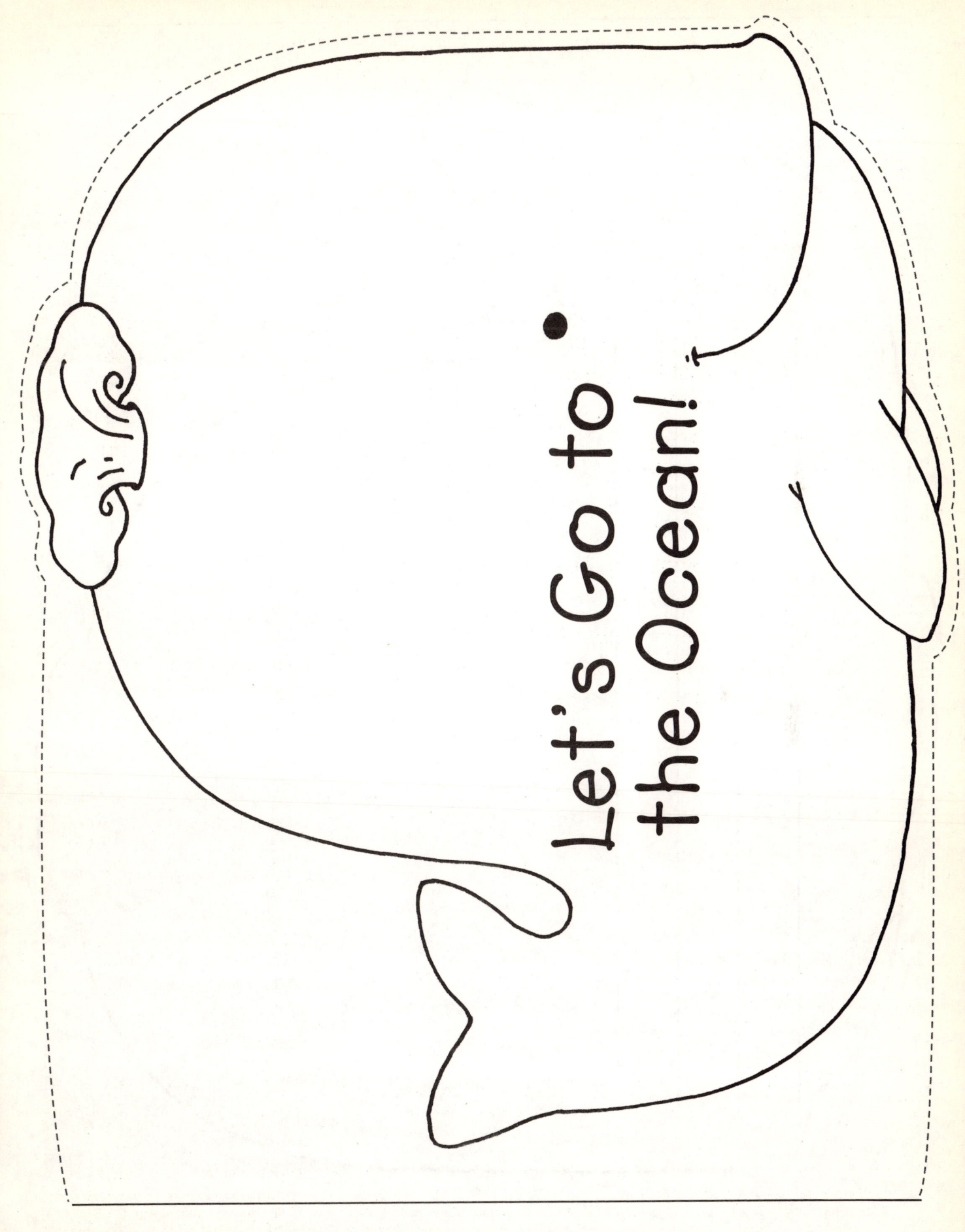

Let's Go to the Ocean!

# The Legend of the Indian Paintbrush

### by Tomie dePaola (Putnam, 1988)

After reading an inspiring Native American tale, children write about their own dreams for a better world.

**Themes:** Dreams, Perseverance, Native American Folklore

## Cover Preparation Idea

1. Photocopy the cover template onto tan paper. Mount it on sturdy paper and cut out. For the back cover, trace onto sturdy paper and cut out.
2. Using a thin marker, add details to the cover.

## Literature

Little Gopher's belief in his Dream-Vision helped make his world a better place. But his goal was not realized immediately. As you read, talk with students about Little Gopher's feelings. Ask students how they think he feels when the warriors go off without him and when he paints beautiful renditions of their stories and adventures. When Little Gopher's Dream-Vision is realized, his people change his name to He-Who-Brought-the-Sunset-to-the-Earth. Ask students how they think he felt about that. After the story, review the range of feelings Little Gopher experienced while he worked toward fulfilling his Dream-Vision.

## Writing & Art

Photocopy the student writing page onto tan paper. Explain that in the story, the Dream-Vision for Little Gopher explained how he would make the world a better place. Ask students to imagine a Dream-Vision for the world. Invite students to close their eyes and then evoke images of a better world. What is it that they see? Their Dream-Visions may be personal or family oriented. They may be visions of a better school, community, or world. Write on the board: **"My Dream-Vision is _____."** Have students complete the prompt by writing words that describe their visions. Remind students of Little Gopher's perseverance. For an extra challenge, have children describe how they might help their Dream-Vision come true.

### Beyond the Book

- Explore other Native American legends and launch a unit on Native American cultures.

- Read stories of others who followed their dreams. Talk about the courage it takes to do something that seems like an impossible task.

**Book Links:** *The Girl Who Loved Wild Horses* by Paul Goble (Bradbury Press, 1978). A young Native American girl courageously leaves her tribe to follow her heart. *The Legend of Bluebonnet* by Tomie DePaola (Putnam, 1983). A young Native American girl sacrifices her most treasured possession to help her people. *Snowflake Bentley* by Jacqueline Briggs Martin (Houghton Mifflin, 1998). This is the compelling story of Willy Bentley, a man whose passion was his gift to the world. His work forever changed the way we look at snow.

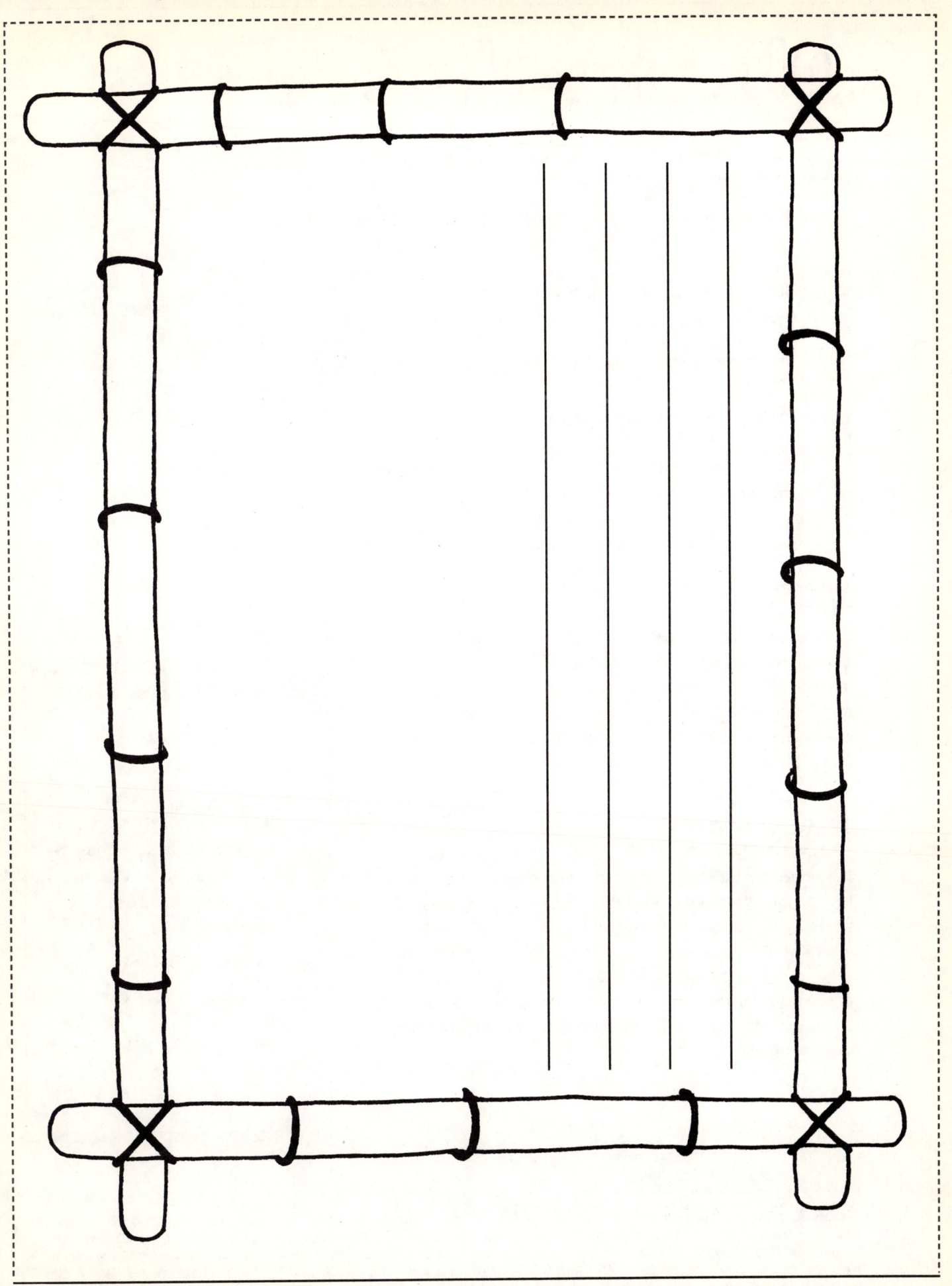

# Oh, the Places You'll Go!

### by Dr. Seuss (Random House, 1990)

Find out where children would go if they could go anywhere in the world.

**Themes:** Responsibility, Map Skills, Journeys

## Cover Preparation Idea

1. Photocopy the cover template onto white paper. Mount it on sturdy paper and cut out. For the back cover, trace onto sturdy paper and cut out.
2. Using a thin marker, draw passengers in the car windows. As an alternative, cut and glue magazine pictures or student artwork in the windows. Color the cover.

## Literature

Dr. Seuss uses rhyme to tell the story of life's great balancing act. Before you read, explain that this is a story about taking responsibility. Review with students what it means to be responsible, particularly for your own actions. Provide concrete examples as necessary. As you read, pause to ask students what the main character should do. For example, when he's stuck in the perch, what are his choices? What should he do?

## Writing & Art

The narrator describes many interesting and colorful places. Explain that there are many other places to travel. Where would your students like to go? If they could go anywhere, where would they choose? They may begin with **"I will go to_____."** Encourage students to include one reason they chose this particular place. What would they see and do there? When writing is complete, students can draw themselves and other people in their car.

## Beyond the Book

- Use students' travel ideas to launch a map skills unit. Use colored pushpins to mark their desired destinations on a world map. Discuss the different modes of transportation that could be used for each trip.

- Poll the class. Ask: "Who has traveled on an airplane? A train? A bus? A car? A cruise ship? A space shuttle?" Graph student responses and add to a display.

**Book Links:** *Arthur Lost and Found* by Marc Brown (Little, Brown, 2000). Arthur and Buster miss their stop when they fall asleep on the bus. With no money for return fare, they must rely on their ingenuity and the kindness of others. *Crossing* by Philip Booth (Candlewick, 2001). Children will marvel as the cars of a train roll through the railroad crossing. *Miss Spider's New Car* by David Kirk (Scholastic, 1999). Miss Spider goes on a shopping spree, hoping to find a new car. *Rattletrap Car* by Phyllis Root (Candlewick, 2001). In repetitive text, the children convince Poppa to take them to the lake, but he's not sure they'll make it in his rattletrap car.

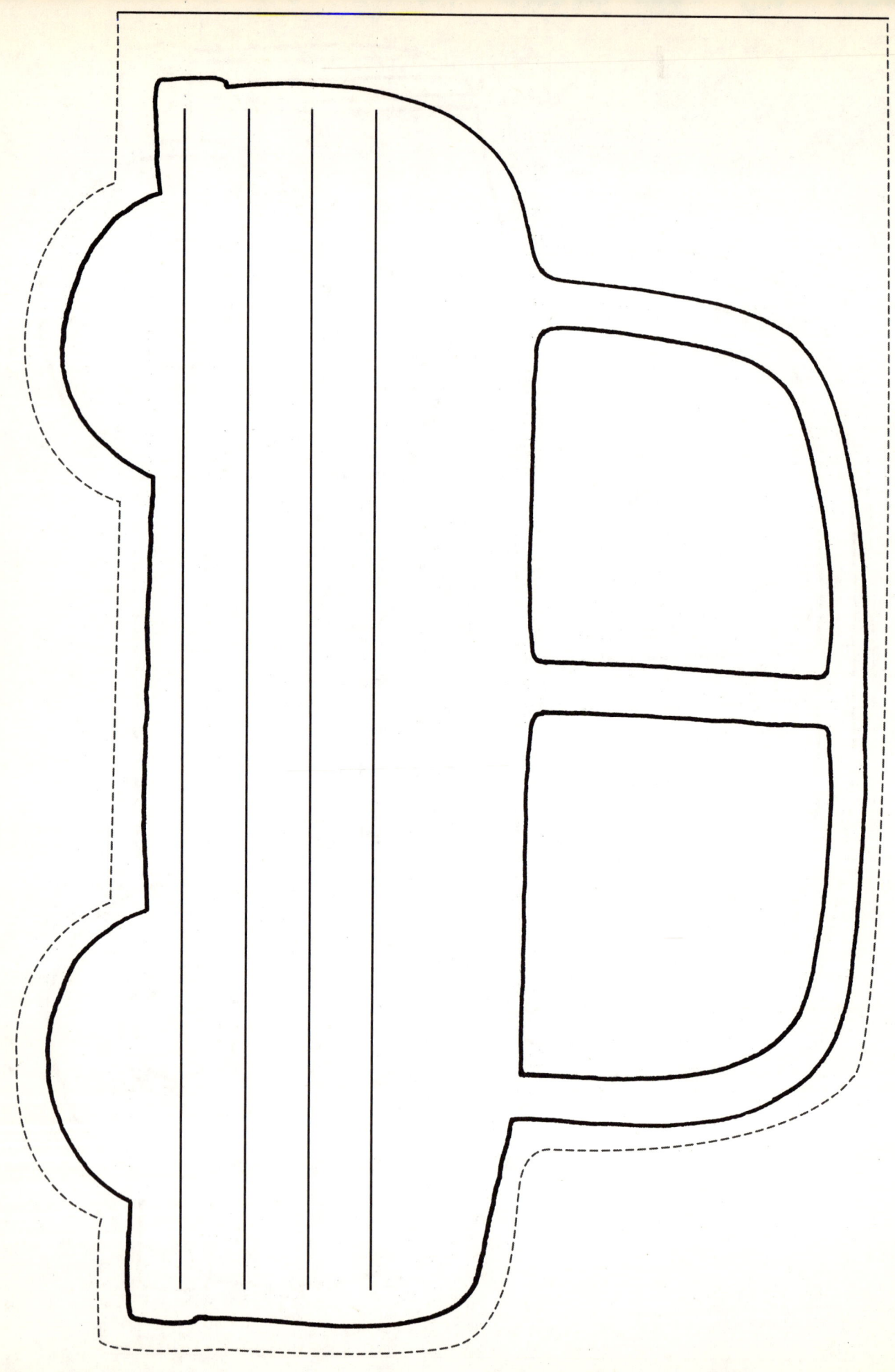